"However, THE THING (Whatever it was) DID NOT run away from me as you might expect, INSTEAD IT RAN TOWARDS ME, then disappeared into the darkness of night... And then it was gone, out of sight but not out of mind; LEAVING BEHIND A MEMORY THAT WOULD LAST A LIFETIME!!!"

The Author

THE OHIO MONSTER

MY PERSONAL ENCOUNTERS WITH BIGFOOT
DAVID WALKER

authorHOUSE®

AuthorHouse™
1663 Liberty Drive
Bloomington, IN 47403
www.authorhouse.com
Phone: 1 (800) 839-8640

Published by AuthorHouse 07/09/2018

ISBN: 978-1-5462-3168-4 (sc)
ISBN: 978-1-5462-3167-7 (e)

Print information available on the last page.

Contents

DEDICATION

This book is sincerely dedicated to all the men, women and children who have actually seen the tall, hairy monster known as Bigfoot or Sasquatch; but were afraid to come forward with their stories for fear of ridicule. I've been there where you're at and I feel your pain, trust me. I told my story and was instantly laughed at and ridiculed, as well. But the truth IS THE TRUTH and THE TRUTH **MUST BE TOLD**, whether it's believed or not! This is MY STORY and I hope that someday, ***YOU WILL HAVE ENOUGH COURAGE TO TELL YOURS, AS WELL!***

ACKNOWLEDGEMENTS

First and foremost, all praise & glory goes to my Heavenly Father for setting the events up in this book many years ago. Unbeknownst to us, as individuals, His plan and purpose supersedes anything that we may have planned for our own lives; causing His will to be accomplished in the end. Again, thank you to the Blessed Heavenly Father, the Lord Jesus Christ & the Holy Spirit for allowing me this unique opportunity.

Also, a very special Thank You goes to my wife, Barbara, for being the primary inspiration behind this book. Having just completed one of her own, a publication called *"Panther and Me,"* she encouraged me to write a book about my experiences with Bigfoot. She said it should do really well because the paranormal field is really hot right now. Had it not been for her constant prodding, I seriously doubt this book would have ever made it off the kitchen table. She truly is a Super Woman and I thank God for her everyday!

Another Super Thanks goes to David Bakara, Owner of *"Expedition Bigfoot, The Sasquatch Museum,"* located in Cherry Log, Ga. The very moment I met this man I felt a special kinsmanship, like we had known each other our entire lives. I just knew there was something special about him and I was definitely, right. Knowing we both felt the same way about Bigfoot, I asked David if he would consider reading my book called *"The Ohio Monster,"* and write a Forward about it afterwards? He said, "Sure, I'd love to," however, I didn't expect him to say some of the things he did about it. To say I was blown away by the content would be an understatement of the highest degree. All I can say is, Thank You, David, for those kind and thought provoking words.

And last but certainly, not least, a very special Thank You also goes to David's store assistant, Sybilla Irwin. When I say this lady has a super artistic talent, I'm not kidding you at all! Sybilla can draw anything you ask and make it look better than anyone else, bar none! And when she starts drawing pictures of Sasquatch, her already wonderful talent jumps to a whole new level...OFF THE CHARTS! Miss Irwin has the very unique ability (as she listens to you describe your encounter) of being able to see inside your mind's eye and can capture the exact image (almost every time) that you want displayed on paper. Unbelievable or should I dare say the word "Supernatural," much like the creature itself (my opinion, not necessarily her's).

In one of those "supernatural" moments I just mentioned, she actually drew the exact outline of my friend George (the other boy in the tent with me; displayed on the Front Cover of this book) just like he appeared during that time, to a tee. George wore a particular haircut and she nailed it, folks, without ever seeing a single picture of him. Eerie *Twilight Zone* music playing now...do, do, do, do, do, do, do, do...etc.

Seriously, if you're looking for an artist with plenty of experience, creativity and an eye for detail, this lady is your ticket (she can be contacted at *Expedition Bigfoot, The Sasquatch Museum* , Cherry Log, Ga). Thank You, my friend, for making the outer wrapping of this special "One of a Kind" publication - so beautiful. May God bless you for it!

I also had encouragement from my lovely daughter, Heather Walker Mann, who on more than one occasion would say to me that I needed to start up "A Bigfoot Conference" of my own someday. And I still might, although, I haven't just yet; too busy writing books right now... lol! Thank you, honey, for all your kind and diligent support. I have never forgotten our phone conversations about the subject. We had some good ones, didn't we?

Also, I would like to thank Patti Lawver Grewell for encouraging me to start up a writing career. Patti was a classmate of mine from Newcomerstown High School, of which I included a story about in this book. Patti and I recently found each other on Facebook and have been corresponding back & forth. During our conversations she remarked about my writing talent. She said I should consider writing a book sometime because I had a way with words. So this "acknowledgement" is my way of saying "Thank You" to my dear friend for believing in me.

And thanks to everyone at Author House publications for your patience with me throughout this process. I know I wasn't always easy to work with, but you all did a fantastic job of accommodating me, nonetheless, and seeing me through some difficult time periods.

FORWARD

Take The Journey!

After nearly 40 years of research, witness interviews, and on-site investigations, my opinion on where these creatures come from, has slowly changed. From lost ape, to relic hominid, and finally the inevitable conclusion that these creatures are far more than any of us have ever guessed. In a day of re-examining the same evidence over and over, Mr. Walker's book hits the nail squarely on the head! His unique and honest style is easy to read and unambiguous. Get ready for a healthy dose of truth about these lost "cousins". Put away your preconceived ideas, and high school science teachings. You're about to take a ride into the REAL world of Bigfoot!

David Bakara
BFRO investigator
George, Florida
Owner
Expedition Bigfoot
The Sasquatch Museum

THE INTRODUCTION

Bigfoot, the creature you see on the front cover of this book, needs no introduction. He has been the subject of so many pieces of literature, videos, dvds & *You-Tube* posts that it's hard to comprehend. For a creature that isn't supposed to exist according to science, he sure has a huge following! Bigfoot and others like him are called cryptids; meaning an animal or creature whose existence is questionable because of a lack of evidence to support they are real. Examples of cryptids include the Lochness Monster, the North American Bigfoot, the Australian Yowie, West Virginia's Mothman, the Dover Demon, the Jersey Devil, the Goatman, and one newcomer called the Chupacabra (a vampire-like creature that supposedly has been attacking livestock and sucking the blood out of them).

The study and search for cryptids is called cryptozoology, performed by those who wish to evaluate the possibility of these so-called "mythical beings" existence. However interesting these all are, the one we'll focus our main attention on herein will be the North American Bigfoot or, as the Indians like to call him, Sasquatch (the names are interchangeable and refer to the same being).

Bigfoot has many different names, mostly due to the geographical area the sightings occur in rather than describing a different entity. For example, the name "Sasquatch" (given to him by the Native Americans) means "big hairy man." Interestingly, the Indians HAVE NEVER questioned the creature's existence and stories about him have been passed down from generation to generation in their oral legends. They regard the Big Hairy Man as a sacred being, calling it their *great elder brother."* They also believe it borders between two states of consciousness, animal and human; attributing special powers to the bipedal entity.

Some tribes also regard Sasquatch as being more spirit than physical, which I find rather interesting. This 'Spirit Part' may explain why Bigfoot is so highly elusive and can detect (perhaps through telepathic means) when people are out to do him harm. Therefore, he uses these 'special abilities' in order to evade his would be captors. However, he is also 'Part Physical,' as well, leaving behind scant traces of his presence in the form of footprints, blood & hair samples, and in rare cases, photographic and or video evidence.

Cryptozoologists (those who study these 'questionable' creatures) have been on the trail of Bigfoot since the late 1950's when multiple reports of giant footprints began emerging out of Northern California. In 1958, a bulldozer operator named Gerald Crew found several large footprints around his construction site in Del Norte County, California and had a friend make plaster casts of them. The story gained lots of attention after being published by the *Humboldt Times*; after that it was picked up by the *Associated Press* where it drew international acclaim. Thus, the legendary creature called "Sasquatch" by the Indians received another new name, "Bigfoot," describing its huge feet. Since then the B.F. (short for Bigfoot) craze took off with more and more sightings reported not only in the U.S., but over the ENTIRE WORLD, as well.

Here in North America, the Pacific Northwest has been home to the highest concentration of B.F. sightings to date. States such as California, Oregon, Washington State & the Canadian Provident of British Columbia have been a virtual "hotbed" of B.F. sightings in recent years. So popular is the creature in this particular region that a highway has been named in his honor. The U.S. National Forest Service has named a remote stretch of California Route 96 as *"Bigfoot-Scenic Bi-Way."* It begins in Willow Creek and winds northward for about 89 miles till you reach the town of Happy Camp in Siskiyou County. As a point of reference, the most famous piece of alleged B.F. evidence to date (the 1967 Patterson-Gimly film) was captured at the highway's midpoint, just outside of Orleans near Bluff Creek. There have also been many other alleged B.F. sightings in this area, too, with a large percentage of them occurring in the vicinity of Willow Creek.

Here in the vasts forests and woodlands of the Pacific Northwest there is ample room for the creature to dwell, yet be in a secluded niche far away from humans. And believe it or not, there is more unexplored territory in this region than one might expect, making it a safe haven for the cryptid to live. However, Sasquatch is not just limited to the Northwest alone, but has also been seen in every single state of America, from the thick forests of New England over to the tall, thick Redwoods of California and everywhere in between.

Internationally speaking, in Russia they call the tall hairy beast "Yeti," or "The Abominable Snowman." As you probably know, the U.S.S.R. is home to the world's most vast stretch of real estate on the planet, with untold hundreds of miles in between cities. Like the Pacific Northwest, here there is ample room for the creature to roam undetected, far away from civilization. Up here in the colder climate the creature's fur is mostly white, leading to its name, "The Abominable Snowman." They look very much like the North American B.F. and beside their white fur, are otherwise difficult to tell apart.

Igor Burtsev, a doctor of historical sciences & director of the *International Center of Hominology* (NGO), says that there are reports of people seeing these large hairy beasts ALL OVER Russia. He recalled one of the more recent sightings by a 30 year old man as a somewhat, typical case. Apparently, while camping out with a large group of teens in the mountains, the man allegedly encountered a tall, hairy figure at night. Now, he's too scared to venture back into the woods.

Some believe that Sasquatch and others like him over the world descended from a giant hairy ape called *Gigantopithecus*, which used to roam the Asian Continent thousands of years ago before it "supposedly" became extinct. This giant ape has been described as a 7 to 10 foot tall black hairy primate who, for the most part, favored seclusion. Some researchers believe this may be the same entity people are claiming to see today known as "Bigfoot," Sasquatch and the Yeti. However, the reader is encouraged to wait until this book is finished before drawing your conclusions based upon this particular assumption. In other words, don't put the cart before the horse.

In Australia the creature is called "Yowie," a hominoid type being described as looking more like a primitive human than a beast. Reports of this cryptid have been circling there for thousands of years, just like the legend of Bigfoot over here by the Native Americans. In Mongolia, the creature is called Almas, described as a large hairy bipedal humanoid. They believe it's a cross between a human and an ape, but just as elusive as the other beasts from Asia and Eastern Europe.

In Florida, Sasquatch is called "Skunk Ape," a name describing the horrible stench associated with the creature. This putrid odor has been described as smelling like lindberger cheese, rotting wet socks and or sulphuric acid. The harsh odor may be attributed to the locations the beast hangs out in, such as methane-packed bogs, deep secluded swamps, creeks, etc. and etc. Obviously, we're dealing with a creature here that favors seclusion and doesn't like to be bothered. However, with the encroachment of modern man into his territory, it is probable that we'll be seeing more of this entity in the near future.

Another name for Bigfoot in the United States, especially in the north, is the "Ohio Grassman." Mainly spotted in the Ohio valley (the area surrounding the Great Lakes), I believe this is the same entity I encountered in several places recorded in this book. It seems that Ohio and Western Pennsylvania have had their fair share of B.F. sightings over the years. Although Ohio may not seem like prime B.F. country like the Pacific Northwest, it's nevertheless abundant in agriculture, water sources and big game. It also happens to be the same area where several ancient "so-called" Indian burial mounds have been located (which, among other things; contained the remnants of giant bones, according to old newspaper articles). This particular information will be elaborated upon more in my forthcoming book entitled *"BIGFOOT: THE SUPERNATURAL PORTAL & The Biblical Connection."* Here in the Ohio valley, sightings of a 7 to 10 foot tall hairy Monster called Sasquatch go back hundreds of years and continue to be reported to this very day.

Another favorite hangout of the Ohio Grassman is Salt Fork Lake in

Guernsey County, Ohio. Over the years, this place has been a profound "hotbed" of B.F. activity. Back in the early 1950's as the lake was being built, it's been rumored the county had trouble keeping construction crews on the project because they kept quitting. Apparently, the workers reported seeing tall hairy creatures there and refused to go back. Eventually, the lake was finished and Salt Fork State Lodge was built, a two-tiered mansion located between Cambridge, Ohio and the rural community of Kimbolton. Today, the lodge plays host to annual B.F. conferences and generates lots of revenue in the process. They also sponsor B.F. tours and provide campgrounds for the faithful to reside in while enjoying all the amenities the place has to offer.

The last namesake of B.F. we'll be talking about is called the "Wendigo," a half-spirit, half physical being hailing from the northern woods of Canada. According to Native American legend, they believe this entity has the ability to transform from a human and has very bad intentions. While this sounds preposterous, it is possible that our Native Americans have seen things in the past that make them believe in the quote "supernatural" side of the creature. If true, this supernatural aspect may account for the reason why a body or bones have never been discovered of Sasquatch. Perhaps these people (our indigenous relatives) know far more than what we give them credit for.

Unfortunately, for B.F. enthusiasts, the field is saturated with people claiming to have faked B.F. evidence before. Concerning the 1958 B.F. prints found by Gerald Crew in Northern California, apparently they were made by Ray Wallace, owner of the construction company Gerald worked for. His son, Michael Wallace, said his dad had made them to play a practical joke on his employees just for fun. To back his story up with, he even produced the original pair of homemade B.F. shoes his dad used to show to the public. The Wallace confession came as a huge blow to the B.F. community because that was the original evidence which started the whole craze.

In mid 2008, B.F. enthusiast Rick Dyer claimed to have found the dead body of an 8 foot tall, 500 lb. Sasquatch in Georgia. However, after it was unveiled to the public a few months later, it turned out to be nothing more than a fake stuffed, rubber ape costume. Then, in

2014, Dyer was involved in yet another scheme to dupe a gullible public desperately searching for a body to prove Bigfoot's authenticity. This time Dyer claimed he actually shot and killed a real Bigfoot in September of 2012. He then took this alleged B.F. on tour to several cities, netting 60,000 dollars altogether. He later admitted (upon closer scrutiny) that it was a fake. Even after this confession, Dyer still maintained he actually shot and killed a Bigfoot in San Antonio in 2012, but didn't want to take the real body on tour because he was afraid it might get stolen. Ok, whatever! Fool me once but you're not going to fool me a second time around, right?

Even skeptics admit that the perpetuation of hoaxes does little but cloud legitimate scientific research and makes it more difficult for true believers to prove their elusive creature's existence. Another B.F. hoaxer, Rant Mullens, revealed in 1982 that he and his friends had carved giant B.F. prints and used them to fake tracks as far back as 1930 (*Dennett - 1996*). And I'm certain that he isn't the only one who has ever done this before, either. If the truth be known, probably hundreds of people have actually pulled this prank off before with phenomenal results. If true, then how does one tell genuine tracks (if there is such a thing) from fake ones? That's the million dollar question because even experts in the field of anthropology, such as Dr. Grover Krantz of Washington State University and Ivan Sanderson, one of the biggest names in cryptozoology, have reportedly been duped before.

With that being said, wouldn't it be fair to conclude that the whole entire B.F. phenomenon is probably nothing more than one gigantic hoax itself? One would certainly think so, however, even if we concede that 95 % of all purported B.F. evidence turns out to be false (which is probably 'overkill,') there still remains 5 % of it that defies explanation or natural logic. This is the hardcore evidence that keeps Bigfoot alive and true believers on his trail, hoping against all odds that an actual body will soon be discovered. We'll see, but I'm personally skeptical there ever will be, especially if my hunch is right about Mr. Sasquatch being a supernatural entity. Nevertheless, I admit that the majority in the B.F. camp still believe in a natural, physical being such as a wild primate of unknown origin. Time will tell whether I'm right or wrong!

As you can probably see, I could personally care less whether anybody ever finds a Bigfoot body or not. I am a true believer in the creature and am NOT ASHAMED to admit it! You may say, "How can you be so confident in making such a statement, especially considering the probability that 95 % of all proposed B.F. evidence may be nothing more than fabricated junk?" Simple, because I have actually seen this so-called "mythical being" before not once, but twice in my life. And I guarantee you, especially in my first encounter, this was **<u>NO MAN</u>** dressed in a monkey suit (details will be forthcoming in Chapter 1).

The first time I saw the Big Man he was only 5 feet away from me and the second time he was an estimated 200 yards. Neither time did I ever see any white color in these beings eyes! The second time I viewed Sasquatch through a pair of binoculars and could clearly see his facial features, but DID NOT detect any white in the creature's eyes. Humans all have whites in their eyes, apes & monkeys, don't! To me, this particular fact alone was a game changer because that's something incredibly difficult, if not downright impossible to fake. You'll also read about other encounters I had of the monster where I didn't actually see the cryptid, but was left with no other alternative than to concede that Bigfoot had to have been the one behind them. Once you finish reading these bizarre stories, I think you'll agree with my analysis!

For whatever reason, Bigfoot chose me as one of the few people he has made his appearance to and in doing so, completely changed my life. Now, at 57 years old, I am searching for answers I didn't have back in my youth. For example, what really is Bigfoot and why did he choose me to reveal himself to? After much research, plus reading several internet websites and books on the subject, I believe I've found the answer. There is a very good possibility that this rare and elusive entity called Bigfoot, "may be" A SUPERNATURAL BEING! I know that may shock some of you and others may put this book down never to pick it up again. However, that would be a big mistake because you'll be keeping yourself from some truly, astounding information. This book actually provides the foundation for my second book coming out on the subject entitled *"BIGFOOT: THE SUPERNATURAL PORTAL & The Biblical Connection."* Originally it was made to be all one book, but

I had to split it in two because otherwise, it would have been way too long. Although both books are needed, the second one is my personal favorite because that's where I get down to the nitty-gritty of explaining (using both biblical and non-biblical sources) what Bigfoot is in my opinion.

As you begin reading about my experiences in this book, I issue A CHALLENGE to you. TRY PUTTING YOURSELF IN MY SHOES and see these events unfolding as if they're actually happening **TO YOU**, instead of me! I want you to feel the same excitement as I felt, when (as a young boy) I stared directly into the eyes of an 8 foot tall, hairy Monster only 5 feet away! Then join me in a howling snowstorm as I follow Bigfoot's trail for over half a mile until I see the footprints disappear into a small cave (all the while knowing Bigfoot has to be in it). Hunt with me in a treestand as it begins to get dark, then shudder & feel the tingles run up and down your spine as you hear *THE MOST CHILLING, GOD AWFUL CRY* of your entire life made by a creature standing perhaps no farther away than 20 or 30 feet!

That's all I'm going to share with you right now, but hopefully, you get the point! Now do you understand why **I AM A TRUE BELIEVER?** I have had these and several other encounters actually happen to me. You may say, "You sound convincing and all, but do you have any real proof to back up your claims?" Unfortunately, No, I don't! Like most people in my situation, I never expected to see or hear a Sasquatch during those times. Bigfoot doesn't wait for you to be prepared; 9 times out of 10... whenever someone has an encounter, they're not expecting one and therefore, are unprepared to provide any proof. The only thing you have is my word alone and while that may sound lame, it's all I have. There used to be a day when a man's word was good enough, but I admit, those days are long gone!

Trust me, I'm not trying to pull anyone's leg here. The experiences you're about to read REALLY DID HAPPEN to me just the way I tell the story (although conversations may not always be 'word for word'). Nevertheless, I AM A TRUE BELIEVER because I HAVE ACTUALLY SEEN the creature with my own eyes, **two different**

times! And once you read these stories, you'll become a believer, too, with or without any additional proof from me.

So sit back, relax, and immerse yourself in several short stories that will leave your mind *reeling* and your heart *pounding* as you STEP BACK IN TIME with me (47 years to be exact) and **RELIVE *THE TRUE LEGEND of BIGFOOT / SASQUATCH!***

Chapter 1

The Campfire Monster (the 1ˢᵗ Sighting)

I t was late spring in 1972 and school was about to be let out for the summer. That Friday my best friend George and I had made plans to camp out at his house for the weekend. I went home and asked my parents for permission and they said it was O.K. George had been seeing some deer behind his barn and we thought if we camped out there we might get to see them up close the next morning. George said that one buck in particular was growing a nice rack and he wanted me to see the animal's big velvet antlers. Back in those days deer weren't nearly as plentiful as they are now and just seeing one was a big deal. I was so excited I could hardly contain myself. However, the actual sighting I would have that night WOULD NOT be that of a deer, but of an 8 foot tall, hairy monster the locals called "Bigfoot."

Dad dropped me off at George's house, a little 2 story country bungalow about 3 miles south of **NEWCOMERSTOWN, OHIO**. He lived on a road called *"Marlatt's Run,"* named after some famous bootleggers who once lived in the area. George's mother, Alicia, helped us get our stuff all ready and soon we were off heading to the campsite behind the old barn. On our way, George pointed to some Black Widow spiders perched in their webs at the corner of the barn's pasteur. He said, "Whatever you do, Dave, don't let one of them spiders bite you. One bite

1

from one of them Black Widows can kill a grown man within a couple of hours." "Yikes," I said, "thanks for the warning."

As we began setting up camp we put our tent together, staked it down and then proceeded to gather wood for the fire. Once done we lit the pile of brush, but because of dryer than normal conditions it got away from us and the fire quickly began spreading. Frantically, we tore our shirts off and began wildly beating the fire until we had it all put out. Had we not been able to, I think we'd have spent the entire weekend in jail instead of camping out.

Once the fire was extinguished, George suggested we move our camp site further up on top of the hill. "I think we've probably ruined our chances of seeing any deer here in the morning," he said regretfully. "That's alright," I replied, "I'm mostly in it for the adventure, anyhow." "Yeah, me too," he added, as we started gathering wood for our next fire. Now, with darkness creeping in we decided to conserve time by splitting up duties. George would set up the little 'two man' pop-up tent while I continued collecting firewood. This time, however, we poured water around the brush before lighting it. It worked like a charm and soon we were on our way to eating some well deserved hotdogs and hamburgers. Afterwards, we made some s'mores and roasted them on the fire for dessert. Now with our bellies full and satisfied we turned in for the night, but as young boys often do we didn't go to sleep right away. Instead, we laid there talking and joking around with each other way into the late morning hours. The last time I remember looking at the time it was 1:30 a.m.

Just as we were getting ready to fall asleep we began hearing strange noises. A series of sharp twig snaps alerted us that someone or something was walking around outside of our tent. Then it sounded like we could hear someone breathing heavy; with slow, raspy sounding breaths... INHALE, EXHALE...INHALE, EXHALE...INHALE, EXHALE... We turned and looked at one another with frightened faces, trying to figure out what was going on. Then it happened, suddenly someone punched their fist down hard on top of the tent and hit George square on his head. "OMG," I yelled, "what was that?" "I don't know," George blurted out, "but that hurt, man." Then he whispered, "I bet you I know who it is, Dave, my brother Ed up here trying to scare us." I thought, yeah, that must be it; there has to be some logical reason for this because no one else knows we're even camping out. Then POW, another blow hit the tent and smacked me on top of my head, too! "Ouch," I hollered, "quit monkeying around Ed, we know its you" (believing, of course, it was George's older brother). George smiled and said, "On the count of 3, Dave, let's roll out and scare him." I nodded in agreement and on the count of 3, I rolled out and jumped up waving my arms, but it wasn't George's brother I saw, instead it was A HUMONGOUSLY TALL, **BLACK HAIRY MONSTER!** I kid you not, I nearly peed my pants as I stood there in disbelief looking at this horrible thing standing a mere 5 feet away from me on the opposite side of the tent. Apparently, I must have startled him, too, because after raising my hands in the air the big hairy monster took off. However, ***THE THING*** (whatever it was) **DID NOT** *RUN AWAY FROM ME* as you might expect, **INSTEAD** *IT RAN TOWARDS ME*, then disappeared into the darkness of night. Its speed was like lightning, 40 yards was covered in a matter of 3 to 4 seconds [1,000 one, 1,000 two, 1,000 three, 1,000 four]. And then it was gone, out of sight but **NOT OUT OF MIND;** ***LEAVING BEHIND A MEMORY THAT WOULD LAST A LIFETIME!***

At this point in the story I'm sure everyone wants to know exactly what the creature looked like. Obviously, few have ever been this close to a Sasquatch before and I guess I just happened to be one of the lucky ones (if that's what you call being lucky). Anyhow, the huge hairy monster didn't give me long to size him up. At most, all I had was a couple of seconds before it took off for parts unknown. However, it would be two seconds that I would relive over and over again for the rest of my life. Even as I write this, I'm reliving the Unforgettable Experience!

The main part, of course, was the creature's height. I distinctly recall having to look up at it (by at least, 2 feet), not straight on. It was also very broad across the shoulders, too, being more than twice the size of an average man. It also had a 'gorilla type' cone head with part of its face being below its shoulders, plus 'coal black' piercing eyes. When it turned and ran past me, I saw it had a long upper body with shorter than normal legs, plus real long arms. And fast, wow, ***that Thing*** must have covered approximately 40 yards in about 3 to 4 seconds flat! I've never seen anything or anyone move that fast in my entire life, even to this very day.

After the giant hairy creature from the Black Lagoon ran away, chicken George finally emerged from the tent and exclaimed, "OMG, Dave, that was Bigfoot!" "Bigfoot?" I asked, "is that what you call ***that Thing***?" "Yes, now come on," he said (with fear in his voice), "let's get the "blank" out of here before *THAT THING* decides to come back and finish what he started." With that being said, we both took off running down over the hill faster than a couple of track stars on steroids...lol! Our flashlight beams looked like a pair of bouncing vehicle headlights as we struggled to find a path through the briars & thorntrees. George jumped over the fence, but I didn't see it and tripped, flipping over and landed flat on my back (sliding down the muddy bank). Remembering what my friend said about the Black Widow spiders, I hurriedly brushed myself off and made a dash for the house and together we pounded on the door until someone let us in.

George's sister Nancy finally opened the door and upon seeing two boys completely "scared out of their wits" asked, "What's wrong with you guys, you act like you've seen a ghost or something?" "We, we, we, we saw something, alright," George stammered, "but, but it wasn't a ghost, it...it...it was Bigfoot." "Bigfoot," Nancy scoffed out loudly with a chuckle, "what have the two of you been drinking, anyhow?" "No, we're serious," I said, "we saw a big hairy monster and it hit us BOTH on top of the head." "OMG," Nancy exclaimed while laughing hysterically, "let me smell your breath, you guys have to be drunker than a skunk. Wait till Dad finds out you've been drinking, George, you're going to be in so much trouble."

Just then George's older brother Ed came running down the stairs dressed in his pajamas and asked what was going on? Nancy told him and then he began laughing and poked fun at us, as well. I looked at George and said, "You seemed to have recognized that creature, George, have you ever seen it before?" He slowly put his head down and mumbled, "Yeah, about 2 or 3 times, Dave." I said, "Man, why didn't you ever tell me about this thing, I thought we were best friends?" "Because I didn't think you'd believe me, that's why," he quickly blurted out. "Where'd you see it at," I asked? "In back of the barn," he replied. "One night the cows were carrying on like crazy when they should've been asleep. Dad took his rifle down off the wall and we went out to the barn to have a look. When we opened the door, we saw something tall and hairy jump up and run out the back. It ran so fast that by the time Dad raised his gun, it was gone. We haven't seen it since, Dave, until tonight; I swear!" "Wow," I said, "we're going to have to tell somebody about this *thing* so they can come out here and kill it." "No, Dave," George replied, "Dad said that's the last thing he needs is a bunch of people coming out here with guns looking for Bigfoot. Someone might get shot, Dad said it's not worth it!

The next morning at breakfast we told the entire family what had happened the night before. George's Mom, Alicia, spoke first and said to her husband, "John, didn't I tell you I thought it was a bad idea to let them boys camp out here because of *That Thing*?" "Yes," John replied, "but I never thought we'd ever see it again after the barn incident." Then he looked at both of us and apologized for putting us in harm's way. He then asked us if we would be willing to go back up on top of the hill with him after breakfast to have a look around? Sure, we said, let's hurry up!

As we began approaching the tent John spotted the first track and shouted, "There's one boys, do you see it?" We quickly walked over to it and bent down on one knee to examine it more closely. You could tell we were amateur B.F. investigators because we didn't have anything to measure the track with nor did we have any plaster paris to make any casts with, either. Pretty dumb, huh? Nevertheless, John was both a hunter & a tracker who estimated the footprints to be around 15 inches long and about 7 inches wide. One strange anomaly was that the track only had three toes, which I thought to be rather odd. However, John said that the tracks they saw behind the barn only had three toes, as well. I confessed to not knowing much about B.F. tracks. "That's o.k., Dave," John replied, "we're still learning about this thing ourselves." He estimated the creature's weight to be at least, 600 lbs, based upon the depth of the tracks, which were about 2 inches deep. In comparison, John weighed 200 lbs and his footprints were only about a half inch deep in the same soil. Unfortunately, we didn't have a camera to take pictures of the tracks. Back in them days (the 70's) we only had Polaroid One Minute Flash cameras (which were kind of heavy and bulky to carry around). Sorry, cell phones were still a thing of the future.

I led the way following the direction the creature ran in and found several more footprints. They were spaced about an average of 8 feet apart which we determined by taking "yard" steps to come up with the measurement. That's really far, however, it should be noted that Bigfoot was running during this particular time, too, which accounted for the extra long strides. We probably found about a dozen or so footprints in all, but then where there should have been more in the center of the logging road, they seemingly stopped for no apparent reason. We walked on ahead looking for more tracks or any type of sign that might indicate something had been through the area recently, but only turned up a few stray dog tracks. In comparison, we could easily see our own footprints, but failed to see anything else. I asked John where the creature could have gone? "I don't know, Dave," he said, while kneeling down to examine the last track. Then he said something that has haunted me ever since whenever I think back upon the strange B.F. encounter.

He said, "Boys, I've hunted these parts all my life ever since I was knee high to a grasshopper, and I've never seen anything like this. Tracks don't lie! There should be more up ahead, but there isn't any. It's as if that thing just up and disappeared or something. I don't know what to make of it."

Then he turned and stepped off the distance Bigfoot had travelled from the last track to the backside of our tent. Although not officially measured, he estimated about 40 yards or so. "And you guys say this thing ran that far in only 3 or 4 seconds?" he asked. "Yeah, Dad," George replied, "Bigfoot ran faster than our High School track star Mark McDonald, didn't he, Dave?" I simply nodded my head in agreement. "That's unbelievable," John said, "if I wouldn't have seen these tracks for myself, I wouldn't have believed it." Then he said, "Come on, boys, let's get your stuff picked up so we can get the heck out of here, this place is giving me the creeps." He didn't have to tell me twice, I grabbed as much as I could and then we all headed back down to the house.

While waiting for my Dad to arrive, John began warning me about not telling anyone what I saw last night. I told him, "No problem, sir, I won't tell a single soul." "Do you promise, Dave," he asked? "Yes, sir, I promise," I said, "you can count on me." "Good," he responded, "I certainly don't want anybody coming out here trying to hunt down a Bigfoot that may or may not be on my property. They'd probably be carrying guns with them and, if so, there's a good chance someone could get shot. I don't care if they would happen to find it, a human life isn't worth the price and I'd feel responsible for the whole thing. Do you understand what I'm saying, Dave?" "Yes, sir", I replied. "Like I said before, I won't tell a single soul; Scouts honor!" He nodded his head but I don't think he believed me. That's o.k., because I didn't believe myself. There was no way I could sit on a story this big, I had to tell somebody about it (besides my parents). However, I soon learned who I could tell and who I couldn't. After much ribbing, I eventually followed John's advice. Like he said, "Dave, some things are better left unsaid!" There was a lot of wisdom in those words.

Unbeknownst to me, however, my encounters with Bigfoot were not over with just yet. Later that same year I would once again find evidence of the creature at my brother's place just outside of ***GNADENHUTTEN, OHIO***, at the end of a howling snowstorm.

Chapter 2

On the Trail of "The Abominable Snowman"

The year was 1972 and it was only my second season of going deer hunting. I had high aspirations of becoming a successful deer hunter like my Uncle Homer, who had harvested a nice buck every year except for one the last 10 years (meaning from 1961 to 71). This year he had asked me to go along with him and you better believe, I jumped at the chance. Unfortunately, for both of us, we had to deal with blizzard-like conditions as one of the worst snowstorms I had ever seen hit the area the night before. All Uncle Homer and I did that day was drive around the country roads waiting for an opportunity to see a deer, but we only saw 2 and they were running for their very lives; we never got a shot.

I heard the storm was so bad that day only 8 deer were killed in the entire state of Ohio. Dad had let me take off school to go hunting, but because of the bad weather they didn't have school anyways. Nevertheless, I wasn't allowed to go again until the weekend. As fate would have it, another storm was scheduled to hit then, too. Knowing conditions were going to get rough, I had Dad take me to my brother Bob's house on Friday night so I could go hunting with him the next day.

Saturday morning (the last day of deer gun season that year) dawned white and cold with another 4 inches of snow blanketing the ground and more still falling. When my brother saw it snowing so hard and found out the temperature was only in the mid-teens, he opted not to go and wished me good luck. I got my gear all ready and began trudging out through the deep snow, "Burrrrrh... it's cold," I said to myself; hope this is going to be worth it. Little did I know the kind of impact those words would end up having! I finally spotted a decent looking deer track and began following it. Soon I spotted a few others and then I lost track of the original one. I remember thinking, wouldn't it be cool if I shot a big buck while my brother was home in bed sleeping? However, as previously mentioned, the weather was against me with the windchill factor nearing a bone chilling 10 degrees below zero, so it was no picnic being out there in those type of conditions. I pulled my toboggan hat down over my ears and kept my head lowered as I battled the freezing wind, cold and snow looking for more deer sign.

As I continued walking slowly and studying my surroundings (a form of deer hunting called "Still-hunting"), I found a unique set of tracks with blood dripping on each side of them. Being the opportunist that I am, I began following them up one hill and down the other until I came to the place where the deer had fallen, but was disappointed to find out that the hunter who apparently shot the deer had already claimed his prize. So much for trying to cash in on what appeared to be an amazing opportunity, I thought. So off I went again, trying to act like Hiawatha, the famous Indian hunter. I slowly started making a big circle which, I believed, would eventually lead me back to a particular spot I wanted to hunt close to my brother's house in the afternoon.

My brother Bob had just recently purchased this beautiful piece of property (an 80 acre farm with a huge house, 2 big barns, a blue Massey Ferguson tractor and a couple of mobile home trailers) for the rock bottom price of just 26,000 dollars. A steal back then and unheard of by today's standards; the place was located about 3 miles southwest of ***GNADENHUTTEN, OHIO***, on County Rd. 10. The land was a hunter's paradise and Bob had just planted his first crop of corn that year. He said he had been seeing some deer quite regularly in the cornfield as he was coming home from work in the evenings. The circle I was telling you about earlier would eventually lead me back to that spot where I planned on taking a lunch break and do a little stand-hunting until dark. However, I never made it that far and for good reason.

As I was slowly meandering back toward the house I came upon some tracks in the snow that completely caught me off guard. At 12 years of age I was certainly no expert when it came to deciphering tracks, however, I knew enough to know that they weren't human or regular animal tracks. These tracks were eerily similar to the Bigfoot tracks I had seen in early summer back at George's house just south of **Newcomerstown, Ohio**. They were just as long in length (about 15 inches), too, and even had the same 3 toed configuration as the first creature had, as well. But what were they doing here nearly 10 miles away, I wondered?

I knelt down and carefully examined them. Once more, I didn't have anything to measure the tracks with or to take pictures. However, I didn't expect to see any Bigfoot tracks that day, either. When I started hunting around 7 a.m. it was still snowing hard, but had tapered off somewhat by now. The B.F. tracks I was looking at must have been made within an hour because just a little snow remained in the tracks, meaning they were very fresh. I also noticed the B.F. tracks went down deeper into the snow than my own boot tracks, indicating the creature that made them weighed far more than I did. I estimated its weight at 600 pounds or more, the same as the one earlier that year. There was approximately about a foot of snow on the ground that day and roughly 4 inches of snow remained under my boots compared to about 2 inches under the B.F. tracks. Since the prints were still fresh I decided to follow them to see where they would lead. I wasn't afraid like the first time because it was broad daylight out AND I was carrying a 12 gauge shotgun loaded with a big 1 oz. *Super X* deer slug. Now let me see the old boy, I mused, and I'll blast him away to kingdom come!

Feeling brave, I set out following the humongous looking footprints in the snow. Here I was, a mere 12 year old boy ON THE TRAIL of **"The Abominable Snowman!"** What if I get lucky and am able to shoot the monster, I wondered, people will remember my name forever. I envisioned my name in newspapers and even thought I might be offered a cash reward for bringing in the elusive being, as well. Who would believe this, I wondered? As it turned out, not many.

I followed the creature's tracks like I still-hunted for deer, taking 3 or 4 steps at a time, stopped, then listened for any sounds or to catch a glimpse of movement. At one time I thought I saw something in the distance, but couldn't be absolutely certain. I eventually came to a barb wire fence, but noticed that the tracks continued straight on onto the other side. Based upon the footprints, it seemed the creature had continued walking like the fence had not been an obstacle in its path. That's quite unusual, I thought, you would think that there would be some type of sign indicating the creature had jumped over the fence, but that didn't seem to be the case. Anyhow, I must have walked another 60 yards or so until I noticed the tracks led into a small cave in an unusually large mound of dirt (about 7 ft. high). However, the cave entrance itself was smaller than I had anticipated, measuring only 3 feet in diameter. Also, there were briar branches dangling over the small hole with snow still freshly laying upon them. I stood there for a moment scratching my head, wondering how in the world a 7 to 8 foot tall Sasquatch (if indeed, that's what it actually was) could have gotten into that cave without first knocking off the snow on the briars above it. Yet as George's Dad, John, had once declared, "Tracks don't lie," and the creature's tracks clearly went into the cave. "Hmmmmm," I thought, "that's really strange."

Just then *A FOREBODING FEELING* came strongly over me, almost like the creature inside that cave was trying to communicate with me in a telepathic way. I thought, you big dummy, what if Bigfoot is in there right now planning on attacking you? What if he comes charging out of there with his arms raised and growling real loud? Are you going to be able to keep your composure long enough to stand there and kill the monster? What if you freak out and drop your gun in the snow, then what? The answer to these questions seemed quite simple to me; RUN, David, RUN, RUN as fast as you possibly can back to your brother's house and never look back. Why? Because Bigfoot might be chasing you! I kid you not, after this *larger than life* feeling came over me I didn't do anymore exploring. I simply followed my instincts and got the heck out of Dodge as fast as my legs would carry me and NEVER DID LOOK BACK!

By the time I got to my brother's house I was soaking wet and hotter than blue blazes. When Bob saw me, he thought I had shot a deer and needed his help in dragging it back to the house. "Didga get him," he asked? "How big is he?" "No and no," I replied, "I didn't get a deer." "Then why are you so hot and sweaty for?" "Because I saw a bunch of Bigfoot tracks," I said. He said "What? Bigfoot?" and then began laughing so hard I thought he was going to pass out. Once he regained his composure Bob asked, "Are you sure it wasn't just somebody's big boot tracks that you saw?" "Yes," I said, "Now come on and I'll take you back there and show you." "No, No," Bob said, "I don't have time for such nonsense, David, or should I call you, "The Great White Bigfoot hunter" and then erupted into more laughter with his wife joining in, as well.

Obviously, my brother didn't believe my story and neither did anyone else, not even my own Dad. Dad told Bob, "Don't believe David, he tried telling us he saw one of those things earlier this year, too. I think he just likes making up stories so he can get more attention for himself." Bob replied, "I don't know about that, but I do know one thing, there aren't any Bigfoots running around on my property or anywhere else around here, either."

Nevertheless, I knew what I knew, even if no one else believed me or not. Like the old saying goes, "SEEING IS BELIEVING", right? And no one was going to talk me out of it. But now with two dramatic B.F. encounters practically back to back in the same year, I began to wonder, "What in the world is going on?"

Chapter 3

What in the World is Going On?

Looking back I have to admit, lightning seemed to have struck twice back there in 1972 with two extreme Bigfoot encounters back to back. What are the chances of that ever happening again? Slim to none I would imagine, right? My young mind was reeling, was it even safe to go back into the woods again? After the first B.F. encounter, I admit to being somewhat timid of going into the woods by myself. However, after talking to several people, including elder members of my family, they persuaded me to face my fears and go for it. My Uncle Homer told me I'd probably have a better chance of hitting *"The Ohio Lottery Jackpot"* than seeing another Bigfoot creature again. He said that while he believed my story, he had never heard anyone else say they ever saw a Bigfoot in the woods before. Therefore, I concluded, my first encounter at George's place must have been a fluke or a "once in a lifetime" thing. I decided to face my fears and go back out into the woods again because that was my passion. I used to imagine myself being like Grizzly Adams, living far back into the wilderness with a big grizzly bear as my companion, braving the elements while living solely off the beautiful land.

I started going back into the woods again with my Dad squirrel hunting and then more times with my older brother Bob. We never saw a Bigfoot, track or anything resembling there even was such a thing; so I tried real hard to forget about my B.F. encounter. I continued enjoying the outdoors without incident until that final day of the 1972 Deer Shotgun Season in Ohio.

After the deer season encounter of seeing the monster's tracks, Dad sat me down and tried talking me out of my B.F. experiences. He said, "Son, sometimes people think they see things in the woods that they don't really see. You might have been fooled by the dark shadows of the forest or perhaps some rare type of animal that you've never encountered before, but it wasn't a Bigfoot, son, trust me. I've hunted in the woods all my life, both during the day and at night and I can honestly tell you, I've never seen or heard about such a creature before. And I never want to hear you talk about it ever again, you hear me?" "Yes, sir," I responded, "I hear you loud and clear, Dad." I felt like an unwanted child, like my words and opinions didn't matter, just the words and opinions of others much older than me. Ok, I thought, I'll play this little game of yours because you guys are my adoptive parents, but I'll never forget about my B.F. encounters. NO-ONE, not even my close-knit family was going to talk me out of them.

"Trust me, if you ever happen to see one of these creatures UP CLOSE and *feel the chilling adrenaline rush* associated with it, **YOU'LL BE A BELIEVER FOR THE REST OF YOUR LIFE!**" *The Author*

After seeing the movie called, *"The Swamp Thing"* in the late 1960's, I confess to being afraid of monsters. I remember (as a child) laying in bed watching the large hairy monster trying to abduct a young girl who was getting ready to bathe herself in a small lagoon. That particular scene frightened me so much that I had nightmares about it afterwards and imagined that *The Thing* was after me, too! Little did I know or imagine at the time that one day that nightmare would eventually come true. I told my parents about it and they said not to worry because the movie (that produced the dream) wasn't real. So I believed them, that is until my 1972 encounters with Bigfoot! After my encounters, Mom said I was just one of those type of boys who had a very vivid imagination. I responded by saying, "But Mom, how can so-called "imaginations,"

BREATHE HEAVY, hit you on top of the head and create tracks on the ground to follow?" She just turned herself and pretended to be busy saying, "I don't know, David, you'll just have to talk to your Dad about it." Well, I had already been down that road before and wasn't about to go there again, you know? That would be akin to beating the proverbial "dead horse" over and over with no results.

But there was still one question that lingered in my mind that I couldn't resolve no matter how hard I tried, "What really were these creatures?" Mom and I had recently started going to church and I had gotten "saved" during a revival. However, there were still a lot of things I didn't understand, so I began studying the Holy Bible in earnest. While doing so, I never saw one single place where it ever mentioned a Bigfoot or anything resembling it. I was afraid to ask my Pastor about it, thinking that, like my parents, he might think I'm crazy or something. So I refrained from being ridiculed by the older establishment and decided to do my own research on the subject. However, as life so often does, I got caught up in other things and my attention was diverted away from my B.F. encounters. Girls, school activities, sports, friends, the C.B. radio craze, cars, television, etc. and etc. took up most of my time and I soon discovered there was more to life than a few Bigfoot encounters I had in the past.

Plus, what I didn't mention was that Dad had "grounded" me from going into the woods by myself for awhile in order to give my mind "a rest," as he put it. He said too much "monster stuff" wasn't good for me and I needed to refrain from what he called "wild fantasies." Dad was real good, at times, of making me feel like the proverbial *"Black Sheep"* of the family, however, I truly believe he had my best interests at heart. He was only doing what he felt was right for me at the time, so I can't blame him for his actions. One day one of my friends came over and asked me if I wanted to go for a ride in the country and Dad consented. And no, I didn't see Bigfoot! In fact, I never saw the creature again until I was 25 years old. So what gives, you may ask, did your parents finally talk some sense into you? No, it wasn't that because I still had a few experiences in between the 1972 and the 1986 actual sightings. In some weird way, the "in between" encounters were just as terrifying, if not more so, than the actual sightings themselves. However, the one you're about to read now was the least scary one of them all, but nevertheless, it can still be regarded as an encounter because of the circumstances involved.

CHAPTER 4

BIGFOOT CAME TO THE FOOTBALL GAME

Is this a joke, you may very well ask? Like those ads you see on television about Sasquatch advertising beef jerky or the Bigfoot show called *"Harry and the Hendersons?"* Just how far are you trying to pull everyone's leg, here? No, irregardless of what you might think, the following story is one hundred percent true to the best of my knowledge. And, unlike some of my other encounters, this one had *multiple witnesses*. Now, with that being said, I'm certainly not implying that Bigfoot bought tickets to the game and sat up in the bleachers eating hot dogs and drinking soda pop. However, as you'll see very soon, he did, in his own way, come to the football game. I'll explain more in a little bit.

I'm not exactly sure what year it was, but I think it was somewhere between 1973 - 76. As you may recall, I had my 'back to back' B.F. encounters in 72, so you can imagine they were still pretty fresh in my mind at this time. Dad and I's relationship was on the mend and the last thing I needed was another Bigfoot sighting to complicate things.

By this time, the mid 1970's, nearly everyone in school had heard something about B.F. or Sasquatch, as some like to call him. Charles Darwin's Theory of Evolution was being taught in our schools as an alternative to the traditional religious culture of my day and some of my classmates were being influenced by it. Among other things, Evolution taught that man came from monkeys and that the so-called *"Missing*

Link" (half-man and half-ape) may soon be found, whether fossilized or perhaps, even alive. Some of our teachers believed that if Bigfoot did, in fact, exist, he may be this supposed *"Missing Link"* in Darwin's theory. I never did buy into that bunch of nonsense, but at the very least, it left open the possibility of Sasquatch's existence.

The **Newcomerstown High School** Trojan football team was undefeated all 4 years of my tenure there. They also had a stellar marching band which won many different contests and awards throughout the tri-state area. I can still remember hearing them practice at my house about a mile away and on a good night you could hear the noise for up to 2 miles or more. I personally believe it was the sound of these loud beating drums that prompted B.F. to come to the game that night. Because it's been so long ago, I can't exactly recall which particular team we were playing now. However, I can remember just how loud those drum beats sounded as each team's band competed against one another during the course of the game.

It has been said before that Bigfoot creatures love to "knock on trees" while holding a piece of wood in their hands. Apparently, this is some form of communication they use to communicate with one another. My question is, "Could the loud drum beats that night from the football game have sounded eerily similar to the sounds of "knocking wood" the creature was used to hearing?" I believe it was and was probably the "calling card" that lured Mr. Sasquatch out of his secluded hideaway from across the Tuscarawas River in order to investigate them.

I remember it was a little past halftime into the third quarter of the game when I heard somebody yell "There's Bigfoot, I see Bigfoot down by the river." People began turning around and looking and then someone else hollered, "I see him, too," and then simultaneously people began pouring out of the stands and running down towards the river to catch a glimpse of the elusive creature. My best friend and I were sitting on the High Jump mats behind the goal posts watching the game when this all started. He said, "Come on, Walker, let's go too, don't you want to see Bigfoot?" "No," I said, "you go on ahead, I'm going to finish eating my food, first." "You're crazy," he yelled, "this is a once in a lifetime thing. Now come on, man, we're going to miss him!" He finally quit waiting on me and began running to catch up with everyone else.

The following Monday at school everybody was talking about the Bigfoot sighting at the football game. Some of the teachers were trying to debunk the sighting, saying it was probably just some tall, homeless man walking along the river who had gotten mistaken for Bigfoot because it was so dark. Others were more open minded about the subject like my science teacher, who believed the creature may be the *"Missing Link"* referred to in Darwin's theory of evolution. He encouraged us to be on the look-out for the being and if we ever saw it again, to let him know and he would call in a special group of researchers to investigate our sightings. Well, weeks went by and soon all the recent fervor of the B.F. sighting began to wane. Chalk up another 'elusive' disappearing act for the *mysterious monster* lurking around **<u>NEWCOMERSTOWN, OHIO</u>**.

Just for the record, my best friend (whose name is omitted for obvious reasons), whom I was talking about earlier, said that he didn't personally see the creature when he went down to the river. However, he said he did talk to a few people who did and they said that they saw it jump into the river and cross over to the island. Plus, I heard other classmates say the same thing. I believe someone had to have seen something, because I noticed the throng of people kept on hollering and pointing towards the river as they continued following the creature's path as he attempted to escape toward his hideaway in the hills.

Perhaps this throng of eye witnesses (whom we never knew personally) were nothing more than a bunch of thrill seekers! Or perhaps they just wanted to believe all the hype and mass hysteria of an alleged B.F. sighting! Or perhaps, *just perhaps*, they *REALLY* were telling **the truth**, the **whole truth**, and **nothing but the truth** so help them, God! Who really got the most attention that night? The ***Newcomerstown High School*** Trojan football team (who won the football game) or Bigfoot? LOL!

CHAPTER 5

WILD SCREAMS &
SOUNDS AFTER DARK

Think back to a time, no, one particular night that was the scariest night of your life. What happened that night? Did you see ghostly apparitions? Hear strange noises? Have a weird or strange visitor at odd hours? Did someone play a bad practical joke on you? Maybe someone broke into your house or perhaps you had an untimely brush with death? I used to know a man (he's deceased now) who would wake up nearly every morning only to find out that his furniture had been rearranged sometime during the night before. Imagine waking up to that every morning. Poltergeists? Paranormal activity? I believe these things are real and push the boundaries of the natural realm into the "quote" spiritual or supernatural realm. This is where true science fails because there's no way to prove or disprove such things.

If you haven't guessed it by now, this chapter is going to be about the scariest night of my life. And trust me, I've had quite a few of them in my time. Remember what I said earlier in my introduction, that when you read these stories of mine, try putting yourself in my shoes; see the things that I have seen and hear them, as well. It is only then that you can get the true picture or impact of my experiences.

During my young and carefree days I used to live in a little yellow house just outside the city limits of **_NEWCOMERSTOWN, OHIO_**, with my lovely daughter, Heather. The place was situated on 18 acres and the house and property had a lot of history (I was told). Part of that history involved the old railroad track bed located down in the bottom of our property. Apparently, it had once borne the train that had transported President Abraham Lincoln from Washington D.C., back in 1865, to his original birthplace in Illinois after he was assassinated by John Wilkes Booth. Now that's what you call "real" history, isn't it? The railroad track wound through the shaded wooded valleys of **Tuscarawas County, Ohio**, providing a very picturesque view of the countryside. About a mile from the yellow house this same railroad track snaked through the bottom of a giant hill, wherein a tunnel had been built long ago to accommodate its passage. Every year one of the science classes from *Newcomerstown High School* would take a trip back along the old railroad track to the tunnel in search of fossils along the steep banks. The tunnel, even at that time, was deteriorating rapidly and was mostly filled with water. No telling what kind of critters or spiders were back in there and we were told to stay completely out of it.

I used to sit and daydream about what that old train must have looked like and the people on board. I would envision black smoke rolling out of the top of the stack as it sped along its course toward its destination in Illinois. I would also try to imagine the people's state of mind, having just lost their leader, President Abraham Lincoln. Now, with their commander and chief gone, who would be able to help heal the nation from such a terrible conflict? That was a horrible time period in our nation's past, but those were days gone by and now, back to the present.

I had just been through a very difficult time period in my own life (a divorce) and had obtained full custody of my little girl, Heather. At the time I was working at the Goshen Brickyard in *Newcomerstown, Ohio*. I was a young, single parent raising a beautiful daughter and I thank the good Lord I had a mother who didn't mind babysitting her grand-daughter whenever dad needed some extra rest. The place we lived at had lots of land on which to roam, hunt, ride Atv's or whatever else we wanted to do, plus, it was close and accessible to town, as well. I loved living there for the most part, but I will never forget that one particular night I spent there ALL ALONE for as long as I live. As a matter of fact, that was the night that prompted me to get the heck out of Dodge and find some place else to live. I think you'll understand why in a little bit.

It was a Friday night and to tell you the God's honest truth, I was just 'dog-tired' from all the hard physical labor it takes from working at a brickyard. I decided that I would let Mom watch Heather that night while I took it easy and caught up on some much needed rest. As usual, Mom was more than willing to get to watch her grand-daughter and told me to take my good ole time while relaxing...lol! I went home and put in a movie and sat down to enjoy some much needed R and R. Yeah, right, had I known everything I would have just stayed at Mom's place that night.

Sometime around 8 o'clock in the evening things started getting crazy outside and I had no idea, at first, what was happening. I began hearing strange loud noises, like the high pitch sound of what sounded like a woman screaming...yet somehow I knew it wasn't a woman making the noise. The thought of Bigfoot did cross my mind, but try as I did I couldn't see a thing down in the bottom around the Security light where the sounds were coming from. The sounds then abruptly stopped and I didn't hear a thing for the next 15 minutes and began thinking it may have only been a stray cat passing through the area, so I turned my attention back to the t.v. Then, Aaaaaaaaaaaaaaaaaaawwwwwwwhhhhhhhhhhhhhhhhh... and then 30 seconds to a few minutes later you would hear... ooooooooowwwwwwwwllllllllllllllllllllllllllllllllll... the sounds started up again and this time they lasted longer than the first time. The "aaawwwh & oooowwwllllllll sounds varied timewise but averaged between 10 to 15 seconds each. Then, between the howls you could also hear LOUD SCREAMS that sounded like a woman screaming for her very life, like "aaaaaaaaaaaaaaaaaaaaaaaaaaaaahhhhhhhhh," then again and again. The screams would be for a shorter duration, 6 to 8 seconds each, but would often occur in cessations of 3 to 4 calls in a series. Now you can probably understand why I was so "scared out of my wits," right? And NO, it wasn't a pack of wolves or coyotes howling, either. These sounds were emitted from a solitary creature with a VERY

LARGE lung capacity, trust me. Wolves or coyotes don't come close to these sounds, not even while howling alone! These Monster howls were several decibels 'higher pitched' than a wolf or coyote. Besides, "back in the day" when these events took place, coyotes hadn't yet moved into Ohio and there were definitely no wolves around, either. Good point to consider, huh?

I peered out of my living room window once more to look down towards the bottom to see if I could see anything. The Howls would come and go, much like the Scary Woman Screams, sometimes they would be mixed together and other times they would sound off separately. As I was intently trying to spot something, wouldn't you just know it, the Security light shut off for no apparent reason. Now here I was all alone in the house and it was pitch black outside. Thank God I still had electric in the house. However, now with the Security light off I wasn't feeling too safe, especially with who knows who outside **HOWLING** LIKE A WEREWOLF **on a FULL MOON NIGHT!** I decided to call Mom and tell her what was going on. After telling Mom my story she recommended I come over to her house and spend the night until things calmed down at mine, but I declined. I made up some flimsy excuse why I couldn't, but to tell you the truth, I was just too afraid to go outside. It'd be my luck I would run right into Mr. Bigfoot and I wasn't about to take that kind of a chance. I'm better off just staying right where I'm at, inside, while he's outside, I remember thinking. Just then another series of screams and howls began to erupt, so I put the phone up to the window and let Mom hear the noises. "Did you hear that," I asked her? "Yes," she said, "OMG, David, I've never heard anything like that before." Son, you better call the Police, they need to investigate whatever's going on out there, you hear me?" "No Mom," I said, "I don't want to call the Police; besides, what am I going to tell them, that I've been hearing sounds coming from a Sasquatch or something?" "You don't know that for sure, David," she snapped, "at least let them come out and check things out for you? I personally think someone is out there up to no good." "O.K.," I said, "O.K., I suppose it wouldn't hurt, I'll give them a call, then."

After calling the Police I sat down and began waiting on them to arrive. During this time more howls erupted and they sounded much worse than before. To be honest, what Mom said did make a lot of sense. Besides, I couldn't say for absolutely certain that the noises were coming from a Sasquatch or not. I finally decided I'd check things out for myself and grabbed my shotgun out of the closet to head down towards the bottom, but guess what, my flashlight batteries were dead. There was no way in the world I was going out there without a light!

Then, about 10 minutes later I saw headlights down in my lane and the Police were finally here. I opened the front door before they even had a chance to knock and asked them what took them so long? The Officer replied, "Sir, it has only been about 45 minutes since we received the call to come out. We simply couldn't drop everything we were doing at the time just because you called." I responded by apologizing, saying, "I'm sorry Officers, it's just that I've been so scared out here it isn't even funny." They asked me what was going on and I told them the story. They asked if I'd be alright while they had a look around and I said, yes, but be careful guys; someone or *something* is out there, I swear. They looked at one another with quizzical faces and then proceeded down toward the bottom shining their lights.

About 15 to 20 minutes later the officers came back and knocked on the door. I opened it and they told me they hadn't found anything that looked suspicious or of a criminal nature going on. The other officer replied, "We also checked the railroad gate, but it was locked and secured. We didn't see any sign of tampering or vehicle tracks going around it, so we highly doubt anyone is actually back in there. But just in case you happen to see or hear anything else, by all means give us another call and we'll come back out."

I thanked the officers for their time and went to close the door, but they just stood there. I opened it back up and asked, "What's the matter, is there something you haven't told me?" The first Officer responded, "Sir, just FYI, this isn't the first time we've had to come out here for a call like this." "What do you mean," I asked? He said, "Just speaking for myself, this is the third time I've been out here in this area since I started on the force about a year ago. Now I don't know what's going on for certain, but if I were you and I heard noises like what you've described,

I'd be finding me somewhere else to live." "Trust me, Officer," I said, "it seems like you've read my mind." He chuckled and then they both left.

I immediately called Mom back and told her what the Officers had said. Mom said, "Then that settles it, you and Heather can move in with me temporarily until you find another place to live." I agreed and then thanked her for the offer.

Not long after the Police had left more screams and howls erupted and these sounded much worse than the ones before. You talk about "blood-curdling" screams, Wow, they were so grievous that I remember falling to my knees and pleading the blood of Jesus to keep me safe from all harm. I seriously regretted not taking Mom up on her offer to vacate the property when this stuff all started. I could have saved myself a whole lot of time and trouble. I know what you're thinking, should have listened to Momma, right? Like they say, Mothers know best!

After this series of screams erupted I probably heard 2 or 3 more outbursts and then all fell silent for the night. However, it was now around 1 o'clock in the morning and being totally exhausted from all the night's tension, I quickly fell asleep on the living room couch and never woke up until 9 o'clock the next morning. I bet you can never guess where I went as soon as I woke up? Yep, you're absolutely right, down to the bottom where I heard all the noises at the night before. While checking the area out it didn't take long before I found something very strange to indicate something or someone had definitely been there. Right by my trash can where briar bushes had once stood tall and proud, an 8 foot swath of them had been totally flattened down to the ground for about 40 to 50 feet on BOTH SIDES of my lane. It looked like someone had taken a steamroller through the area, but of course, that was impossible. But who did it and why? What could possibly have been someone's motive for doing something like this, I wondered? I know it wasn't like that the night before because I had just taken my trash out after I came back from taking Heather to her Grandmother's place. This find prompted me to continue looking for more sign which I thought I would certainly find, but I didn't. I admit, no bigfoot tracks were ever found, however, the area was completely covered in railroad cobblestone and looking back upon things this may have hindered me from finding anything else.

After checking with my neighbor's halfway up the hill, they had informed me that they, too, had heard strange noises coming from my place. Apparently (according to them), this wasn't the first time they had heard the noises, either. This led them to call the Police, but they informed us they had already been out to the place and didn't find anything, she said, so we just went on to bed. The lady then told me something that confirmed renters hadn't stayed there for very long in the past, as well. I called my Landlord and told him what all had transpired the night before. At first he acted surprised, but eventually admitted other people hadn't stayed there very long either, complaining of the same thing. I told him about my plans to vacate the property and that he should have the place checked out really well before ever renting it out again. He somberley agreed and we met later that day and he gave me back my full deposit on the place.

Whatever or whoever had scared the living daylights out of me there at the yellow house in **Newcomerstown, Ohio** that night remains a mystery to some, but not to me. I'm pretty certain it was probably Bigfoot, because the screams and howls I heard sounded eerily similar to what others have described as the Calling Card of Sasquatch. Looking back upon the story now, I think I know what might have happened. There quite possibly may have been TWO Sasquatches living in that area because I recall hearing *two different types* of screams or howls that were made. Perhaps one was calling to the other and or vice versa in an attempt to eventually come together...I don't know...but the theory does sound plausible. Irregardless, whatever was going on, those screams and howls will be forever burned into my memory for as long as I live. **It truly was a night that I will NEVER, EVER FORGET!!!**

Chapter 6

The Mudsock Monster (The 2ND Sighting)

The year was 1986 and it had been nearly 14 years since my first actual sighting of Bigfoot/Sasquatch back in 1972 when I was only 11 years old. Although I had a few graphic encounters of the beast in between, for the most part things had remained pretty normal in my life. Dad had passed away in 1983 and I thank God we had rekindled our relationship beforehand. We had a few talks about Bigfoot and he admitted he was sorry for not believing me at the time. I told him, no problem, Dad, besides, it's not everyday a kid comes home and tells you he just saw a Bigfoot! We both laughed and the wounds quickly began to heal afterwards. We spent what would become the last 7 or 8 years of his life hunting and fishing together and it was just like old times, again. I cherish those particular memories and often think back upon them when remembering my father.

After Dad passed away in 1983, Mom sold the house and we moved to the country on a 2 acre lot about 4 miles south of ***Newcomerstown, Ohio***. It was located in a quaint, little rural community called ***"MUDSOCK,"*** on Route 258 (also called "Old Route 21"). I can still remember my Uncle Homer kidding my daughter Heather and me about living out there. He would often end his conversation by saying, "O.K., David, isn't it about time you and Heather go back on home to Mudsock"...and then laugh his silly head off at us. ***MUDSOCK*** derived

27

its notorious name from the olden days when "horse and buggy" used to be the normal mode of transportation (1870's to 1920). The story purportedly says that that particular stretch of road (where Mom & I had put our trailer at) used to always stay wet because of several underground springs in the area. As one might imagine, horse and buggies passing through that part would often get their wheels **stuck in the mud** and they'd have to have the locals hook up to them and pull them out. You could literally say the place got *"stuck"* with the name, no pun intended!

In 1986 I had just switched jobs and was now working at a cardboard factory in Massillon, Ohio. One night I worked a "double shift" and ended up driving home around daybreak. It was about an hour's journey home and being an avid deer hunter I would often pass the time by looking into the fields for deer. As I rounded one bend of the road close to home, I looked down into the bottom of the river to where I had seen some deer at before. There, to my unbelieving eyes, stood a creature resembling "Bigfoot." It couldn't be, I thought, but wanted to be absolutely certain so I quickly pulled off onto the berm of the road and stepped out of the car to have a look. Fortunately, as I did, I also grabbed my binoculars from the glovebox and hurriedly put them upon the beast to tell exactly what it was. Just as I did, it turned and looked directly at me and we both stood there for about 10 seconds staring at one another. However, I got a good enough look at this thing to convince me it wasn't a human in a bigfoot suit. *The Thing* eventually turned to its right and ambled back into the river bottom out of sight. I say "ambled" because it didn't walk like a human, instead it walked more like the creature from the "Patterson/Gimly" film in 1967 called "Patty;" walking with its knees bent the entire time.

This Bigfoot, although just as tall as the one in my 'first' sighting, wasn't nearly as broad across the shoulders as the one back in 1972. Nevertheless, all the rest of him was nearly identical. All in all I would have to say it looked like a much "slimmer" version of the same creature I saw "back in the day." His arms hung down to around his knees and I noticed the creature had shorter legs than the upper torso of its body, which was very tall. I could also clearly see its face and while quite hairy, it wasn't all covered in hair. The bare skin area was light black or dark grey with black piercing looking eyes, not mad or anything, but more quizzical than anything else. Like it was thinking, "What the h..e.."double L" do you think your looking at, man? I also noted I never saw any whites in the creature's eyes as one would normally see in a human's. You can fake a lot of things but that's probably one detail most guys dressed in a Bigfoot suit fail to take into consideration when they're trying to scare someone. I'm not even sure if it can be faked or not, to tell you the truth; but I don't think it can.

I waited a few minutes to see if it might come back out or perhaps peek its head around a tree, but I never saw it, so I started up my car and took off. I wasn't about to wait around too long just in case it had any intentions of trying to sneak up behind me or something. Let's just say I wasn't taking any chances and leave it at that!

You may say, "Why didn't you go get somebody and return later and do some investigating?" Because I had no idea who owned the property and even if I did, what was I going to say to them? Hey, um, sir, I just seen a Bigfoot creature down by the river on your property, would you mind if I go down there and have a look around? Are you kidding me? Folks in them parts of the woods would quickly tell you to get the "blankety blank" off of my property and never come back or we'll be calling the cops or game warden on you! No if's, ands, or buts about it, period!

After that, everytime I would drive by that place I would always look down into that corner but never did see the creature there again. Was it just a fluke or a wanderer in the area? I don't know, but I will never forget the Monster's face I seen through those binoculars. It really did look more humanish than a primate and sort of resembled some type of cross-breeding between a gorilla and a human being, for lack of a better way of putting it.

You may say, "Well, that sure wasn't as exciting as your first B.F. encounter." And you would be absolutely right, but who says every encounter has to be a super, heart-beating and pounding experience? They're most definitely not all alike and while there may be similar parts to many stories, they vary as much as the creature's themselves. I feel that anytime one sees or has an encounter with one of these type of 'rare beings' is super exciting, whether it's a mere 5 feet away or 200 yards away. Irregardless of the distance, if you've ever had an encounter with one of these creatures before, I guarantee you one thing, you'll never forget about it for as long as you live. It's been said before that **"You don't see Bigfoot UNLESS he wants you to see him,"** and I can absolutely vouch for that statement!

Looking at this sighting through a skeptic's eyes, you may say, "At 200 yards, how can you be absolutely certain this thing was a Bigfoot? It was also down by a river early in the morning, too, so it was probably foggy, wasn't it?" Yes, it most certainly was, but not enough to obscure my vision to the point I couldn't make out the creature's outline or its unique features. Remember, I also had a pair of binoculars, too, which aided my vision tremendously. And no, it wasn't a bear standing on its hind legs looking for food, either. Trust me, I'm a seasoned veteran hunter and I know the difference between a bear and a Sasquatch. In other words, this was no case of 'mistaken identity' if that's what you're thinking!

I understand people's skepticism, especially when they've been out in the woods practically their whole entire lives and have never come across a Sasquatch or Bigfoot before. People tend to judge you based upon THEIR EXPERIENCES, not yours! But try to remember, the world is a big place and few have been around its entire surface or have been everywhere upon it. And just because you personally haven't seen one of these eerie, weird and unique beings before **DOES NOT** MEAN THAT THEY DON'T EXIST! More than a thousand eyewitnesses **ALL OVER THE WORLD** "SIMPLY" **CANNOT** BE **ALL WRONG**!

Chapter 7

An Unforgettable Hunting Experience

While still living in the rural community called **MUDSOCK, OHIO** (the place is so small it's not even listed on the map; I had the Cover Designer place it there for your reference), I would often venture off my 2 acre property to hunt a large tract of real estate owned by *Peabody Coal Company* behind our place. I had seen quite a few deer there and had high hopes of tagging one particular buck the locals called "The Legend." So during the summer of '1987,' I had located a couple of what appeared to be "fresh scrapes" during a scouting mission. I felt good about the area and elected to put up a couple of treestands, trimmed a few branches, sprayed everything down and then got out of there until hunting season that fall.

Around the first week of November that year it got very cold one day so I elected to go hunting that afternoon. I thought it would be a good time to try the "double scrape" stand located a scant 100 yards from our property line. Besides, it wouldn't take long to get there, a big plus when you're in a hurry to get to your stand after work. I quickly showered, put on my hunting clothes and set out for a nice quiet, relaxing evening in the beautiful outdoors. However, not long after arriving **I began to "sense" that something wasn't quite right.** I had been on stand for nearly an hour and hadn't seen so much as a bird or even a squirrel frolicking for nuts on the forest floor. Everything was super still and quiet, which made me think about getting down and calling it a night. However, my dedication to the sport made me stick it out until the very end.

Then, about 15 minutes before dark I heard the familiar sound of twigs crackling underneath a creature's feet as it moved slowly in my direction. I stood on the stand and readied my bow as I had done countless times before. Come on to daddy, I said, hoping any minute now I would see the big buck called "The Legend" walk into one of my prepared shooting lanes. I waited and waited and it kept on getting darker and darker. Come on, I thought, what's taking you so long?

Then suddenly, I heard **THE MOST CHILLING, BLOOD CURDLING "SCREAM" of my entire life!** It was so loud and piercing I actually had to cover my ears because of the "high pitch" frequency of the sound (which lasted between 10 to 14 seconds). Whatever or whoever had made that loud cry COULDN'T have been more than 20 to 30 feet away from me, I swear it was that close. I kid you not, I could literally feel the very hair on the back of my neck stand straight up while the creature was screaming. This piercing cry brought back eerie memories of the little yellow house in **Newcomerstown, Ohio**, where I spent the scariest night of my life; all while listening to Sasquatch whoops & howls during the night. The cry itself sounded like the bone chilling "Scary Woman Scream" that I heard that particular night, which sounded like "aaaaaaaaaaaaaaaaaaaaaaaaaaaaaaaahhhhhhhh!" Because of that memory, I pretty much knew what I was dealing with here, another Bigfoot creature. Plus, it had only been about a year since I had the actual sighting of a Sasquatch down by the river only a few miles away. I simply couldn't help but wonder, **COULD THIS BE THE SAME CREATURE?**

With light fading fast I quickly began lowering my bow, but half way down the rope slipped out of my hands and the bow hit the ground with a loud thud. All the tension of the B.F. cry had me shaking like a leaf and I was literally, a nervous wreck. Having forgotten to bring a flashlight with me, I wondered how in the world I would be able to find the tree-steps I had previously installed in order to climb down. I swung my leg around to stand on the first step, but it wasn't there. It has to be here somewhere, I thought, but try as I did I couldn't find it. Panic began setting in and I wondered how in the world I was going to get down the tree? I decided to go the old fashioned way and "bear-hug" the tree while using my weight to slide down. It worked, but just as I was about to lose my grip and fall completely down, one of my boots luckily landed on a tree step, so I quickly descended to the ground unhurt. Looking back upon it, though, things could have easily turned out different. Instead of being safe, I could've ended up laying flat on the ground unconscious from a head injury or worse yet, death itself. I most certainly have the Good Lord above to thank for my safety and give Him all the praise and glory!

Now, once upon the ground the old saying popped into my mind, "You're not out of the woods, yet." Boy, was that ever true! I quickly realized I was now on the same level as Sasquatch and I knew he couldn't be far away, perhaps he was even watching me this very minute. I had to think and think fast, no time for playing around now. Which way was home, I wondered, and once that was determined there was only one thing left to do, run, and run as fast as I possibly could. I remember the thick briars tearing and ripping my hunting clothes as I ran straight towards home, but I didn't care. All I cared about was getting back to my family safely at that particular point. As I came to our property line I jumped about midway high onto the fence, but unfortunately, my boot became wedged in one of the square strands and I simply "COULD NOT" free it. Not knowing whether the monster was chasing me or not, I frantically mustered the strength to pull my foot out of the boot and continued running to the back porch of our mobile home trailer. "Ouch, ouch," I yelped, as briars & stones punctured my foot!

Mom was standing in the kitchen when I entered the door and upon seeing my state of anxiety asked me what was wrong? "Oh, nothing," I said, "Nothing like a blood-curdling scream to get your blood a pumping!" "A blood-curdling scream," she said, "why I heard something like that, too, a few moments ago. What kind of animal do you think it was David," she asked? I said, "Mom, that was no animal, that was a Bigfoot/Sasquatch or whatever you want to call it." "Oh come on, now" Mom snapped, "you're not going to start that stuff up again, are you?" I just gave her that "David look" and she knew I wasn't kidding. "OMG," she uttered, "you mean to tell me there's one of them things out here, too?" I said, "Mom, what else could it have been? Did you hear how long that thing screamed for?"

Before she could answer, the phone rang. It was our next door neighbor wanting to know if we had heard a loud, piercing cry just a few moments ago? I answered in the affirmative and told him my story. "OMG," he said, "I bet you that's what it was alright, because not too long ago I saw something in my backyard next to the woods that looked like one of them creatures. However, before I had a chance to tell for absolutely certain it slipped back into the woods." The evidence was beginning to mount in favor of the creature being a Sasquatch. We must have ended up talking for over an hour, swapping stories about our encounters. After we were done, I told Mom, "Seems like I'm not the only one who has ever seen one of these creatures before." She ended up apologizing to me about not believing me when I was a kid about seeing Sasquatch. I told her not to worry, because I had a similar talk with Dad, too, just before he passed away.

The next morning (a Saturday) I had every intention of going back to the treestand and retrieving my bow and have a look around. However, it was raining so hard I had to forget about it. It actually ended up raining for 4 days straight and I mean, it was pouring down like cats and dogs the whole time, both day and night. At the end of the fourth day it finally stopped and I went out in the morning to retrieve my bow. The bow, a **Black Widow** recurve, was totally ruined. I had just recently bought it, too, but there was no way to retrieve it until the rain had completely stopped. I did recover my boot, though...big deal, right?

You can say what you want to about the blood-curdling scream I heard. You can choose to believe it may have only been a wildcat or perhaps just another hunter in the area trying to scare me or play a bad practical joke. Personally, I believe it was a Bigfoot/Sasquatch being, as you might expect. One thing's for certain...the creature had been seen in those woods before and not *just* by me alone. Apparently, something very creepy and lonely was **prowling around** in the back 40 acres of our little home in ***Mudsock, Ohio***.

CHAPTER 8

A ROCK THROWING
SASQUATCH?

Not very long ago I used to live in a mobile home trailer off of Watson Creek Rd., *Uhrichsville, Ohio,* along with a very close friend of mine named Sarah. One afternoon in late Summer (the month of August), Sarah and I decided on going fishing in a neighbor's lake behind our property. The lake was full of largemouth bass and we would often hold contests to see who could catch the most. For the record, we would use a "catch & release" system to ensure the lake never ran out of fish.

That particular day we decided to go fishing early and arrived at the lake around 2 o'clock in the afternoon. The weatherman had predicted the temperature to fall a little towards the evening and we wanted to be ready when the fish began biting in earnest. After we made our initial casts off the damn of the lake, we sat down on the bank and began chatting while waiting on the fish to bite.

Suddenly and without warning, we noticed A ROCK was thrown into the back of the lake. "What in the world was that," Sarah quizzically asked me? "I don't know," I said, "there aren't any kids back in there that I know of, are there?" "No," Sarah replied, "Jerry's kids (our next door neighbor's) are with their Mom today shopping for school clothes, they're not even home right now." "Then who in the world could be back in there throwing rocks," I asked? Just then another rock was thrown in and this one was much larger, causing huge ripples to cascade across the large pond. "What in the world's going on," Sarah asked me once again? Then she whispered, "You don't think it's Bigfoot, do you?" The timing, I add, couldn't have been more perfect.

Sarah was quite aware of my experiences with Bigfoot. And although she may have been a little reluctant to admit it, I believe Sarah was a believer in the Monster, too. She told me about a particular experience she had one night not long after we first met. She said, "David, whatever that thing was, it scared the living daylights out of me." As Sarah was laying in bed watching t.v., she noticed an enormous figure walk past her bedroom window. For the record, her bedroom window was a good 6 to 6 and a half feet above the ground and she didn't see the person's head; meaning whoever had walked past it had to have been, at least, 7 feet or more in height. Then, to top matters off, she began hearing loud rapping noises on the side of her trailer. Startled out of her wits, Sarah got down out of bed and began pleading the blood of Jesus to protect her from all harm. Not long afterwards, she said, the rapping noises stopped. Sarah told me she was pretty certain that the large shadowy figure she saw through her bedroom window that night was some sort of a bigfoot creature because of its unbelievable size.

As I was beginning to say earlier, the timing of the rock throwing couldn't have been more perfect. Just the night before we had watched a B.F. documentary wherein they had said that one of the things B.F. creatures like to do is throw rocks close to people, in an effort to warn them of their presence. Knowing this beforehand, that was the first thing I thought of when I heard the first rock go splash into the back of the lake, but I didn't want to alarm Sarah. However, she caught on real quick and we both began thinking the same thing, that there may be a Sasquatch back in that tangled mess of briars and swampy ground trying to; in his own way, alert us of his presence and warning us to leave.

Sarah said, "David, I think it's about time you go back in there and check things out." I said, "Are you asking me or telling me?" Before she had a chance to reply, another rock was thrown into the lake, this time it made a big kerplunk sound, being much larger than the previous ones. Sarah then replied, "I'm telling you, with fear etched into her voice." I said, "O.K., O.K., I get the point," and put my fishing pole down and slowly began walking towards the back of the lake.

When I passed the old camper nestled in a bunch of briars near the tail end of the lake, it hit me. No, not a rock, I knew that's what you were thinking. I'm talking about a foul odor that smelled every bit the part of lindberger cheese and or sulphuric acid. The smell was so bad that it literally made me sick to my stomach and I pinched my nose shut in an attempt to keep from vomiting. Yes, it was that bad! I just knew I was in the presence of another Sasquatch, but try as I did, I couldn't see it. In my defense, it was mid August when this encounter took place, so it goes without saying the foliage was very thick and the furthest I could see in most cases was a mere 10 yards. After looking around for about 10 minutes or so I couldn't take the smell any longer and left without seeing a thing. Sarah began motioning for me to come over and the first thing out of her mouth was, "Didga see anything?" "No, I didn't," I said, "but something was back in there alright because the smell just about made me regurgitate." "Well, you know what they say", she mused, "there's usually a strong odor around where a Sasquatch is at." "Yeah, you're absolutely right," I said, and baited my fishing pole up and threw it back out into the lake. "Are you fishing again," Sarah asked with a sigh? "Uh, yeah, that's what we came to do, isn't it," I quipped? "Not me," she said, "I've had enough of Mr. Sasquatch throwing rocks at us, I'm going back home before he decides to attack us or something," and then gathered up her stuff and began to leave. "Besides," she replied, "it's about time for supper, you coming?" "In a minute," I yelled, "in a minute or two."

Not long after Sarah left another rock or perhaps, I should say, "boulder" was cast out into the lake creating a huge splash. This one had to have been at least, the size of a soccer ball, I swear! That was all the encouragement I needed to call it a day and join my friend back home for supper. As I entered the door I told Sarah about the last "boulder" Sasquatch had thrown out into the lake. She said, "It doesn't surprise me any, that's why I told you I didn't want to stay anymore, I figured we'd see more rocks thrown and God knows what else might happen. I think we should stay up tonight and keep an eye out for Mr. Sasquatch should he decide to pay us a visit." "Well," I said, "let's just say I don't plan on doing any late night fishing and leave it at that." We both laughed and then ate supper. I thought about going back to the lake in order to see if I might find the creature lurking somewhere around it, but decided against doing so. I thought if I did, I might accidentally encourage *The Thing* to pay us a visit later that night.

After supper we sat down on the living room sofa and began talking about Bigfoot. Sarah ended up telling me stories about the creature in that area I had never heard of before. One involved our close neighbors, Jerry and Cindy. Their boy, Chipper (who at the time was about 8 years old) had an experience early one morning when he got up to use the bathroom. When he walked by their living room window, he noticed something out of the corner of his eye standing in the backyard looking directly at him. She said he froze at first, but then slowly turned and looked at the creature and described it to his dad the next morning. Chipper said, "It was much taller than you, dad, and to tell you the truth, it looked like a giant wildman with long, shaggy looking hair all over its body. It was really broad across the shoulders, too, like it would make two of you put together. After I went into the hallway and used the restroom and came back out, I peeped outside to where the thing was standing before, but it was gone. It was then that I knew for absolutely certain I wasn't dreaming. Something was out there, Dad, I swear and it scared the living daylights out of me," he said; while being visibly shaken by the incident.

After Jerry heard about his son's encounter with the monster, he and his wife, Cindy sat down and had a long talk. "Do you really think Chipper seen a Bigfoot creature," Jerry asked Cindy? "I don't know," Cindy replied, "but I believe he saw something, did you see how bad he was shaking while telling you the story?" "Yeah, that was pretty noticeable, wasn't it," Jerry asked with a chuckle? "What do you think I should do, go look for this thing," Jerry asked his wife? "I think you should," she replied, and the sooner the better while sign is still fresh. Besides, you owe it to your son to take his story seriously or he may never trust you in the future if you don't. He needs to know his Dad believes in him, even if you don't find anything," Cindy said. So it was settled, Jerry would go look for evidence of the creature in the back 40 acres that surrounded their humble dwelling.

The next day, as planned, Jerry set out looking for something that might prove his son's story the night before. He first looked for footprints in the backyard, but only found some indiscernible depressions that could have been made by anything, certainly not ironclad proof. He then figured that he would probably have to put in some major legwork if he was to give this expedition any serious effort on his part. So off he set for the thick, briar infested back 40 acres, rich in swampy ground and several creeks flowing from the back of his grandmother's property. About an hour into his search as he was fighting his way through a briar infested creek bottom, he noticed what appeared to be a large, faded footprint that looked like a Bigfoot being could have made it. However, it was about 3 or 4 days old and once again, it may have only been somebody's very large boot track, he surmised. He knew he would need better proof than this. Besides, he needed to be one hundred percent certain himself that what he found actually belonged to the creature Chipper allegedly encountered. He wasn't going to lie to his son and say that he saw something when he knew that he didn't. God wouldn't let him lie, he said. He needed absolute, undeniable proof.

He continued his search up the valley and then turned toward the high hill area towards his left while getting close to the end of his grandmother's land. As he was nearing the very end of their property, he saw something that definitely didn't look natural. Upon closer examination, he observed something that looked like a primitive style hut. Made out of large tree branches, Jerry noticed what appeared to be "claw marks" on the branches and the branches HAD NOT been cut, they had been snapped in two. Bingo, this was the proof he was looking for, however, he didn't have anything like a camera or cell phone to document his find. In retrospect, Jerry admitted, he wasn't very optimistic that he would find anything that *significant* or he would've taken his camera along, he confessed to Sarah afterwards. Nevertheless, as he was preparing to leave the site he saw another "quote" bigfoot hut not more than 50 yards from the former one, along with the same type of claw markings as the first one. He couldn't believe his luck and regretted not bringing a camera along with him. He also found a few more large footprints, but like the first ones; they appeared to be very old. However, he knew it was a very large being that had made them, too large to be a man's, he said.

"Wow," I responded, "this is so interesting, how come you never told me this stuff before?" Sarah looked at me and smiled, saying, "Because you never asked, that's why?" I scratched my head in amazement saying, "This is like, so surreal it isn't even funny. You mean to tell me that the same place I go back into and hunt deer at is actually the same place where a Bigfoot creature lives?" "I don't know," Sarah replied, "maybe, does that mean you won't be hunting back there anymore?" "No, I don't mean that, you know me, nothing is going to stop me from hunting back there; it's too good of a spot. Besides, I've never heard of a Bigfoot actually hurting anyone before, so I think I'm probably safe in that regard. Plus, I'm the one carrying a weapon. If I have to, I'll just shoot **"The Thing."** Sarah laughed out loud and said, "Good luck with that one," and we both ended up laughing.

Two people, my close friend Sarah, and our neighbor's son Chipper, had sightings out there where we lived at off of Watson Creek Road, ***UHRICHSVILLE, OHIO***. And although not a sighting itself, Sarah and I had an eerie encounter while fishing in the lake behind our property. I think everybody can agree, rocks don't fly by themselves, someone or SOMETHING had to have thrown them, correct? And what about the putrid smell I had while investigating the rock throwing? What do you think could have caused that, other than a Sasquatch? Plus, this particular area is only a couple of miles west of my brother's old place on County Rd. 10, ***Gnadenhutten, Ohio***, where in Chapter 2 of this book I saw the B.F. tracks in the snow. Is there a possible connection, you may wonder? Is it possible (however remote) that this may have been the very same creature that gave me the 'slip' back in 1972? Or perhaps an offspring? I don't know, but nevertheless, it is a possibility, don't you think?

Remember, folks, HE ALWAYS FOLLOWS THE CREEKS! And there's a bunch of creeks back there in that swampy ground surrounding Watson Creek Road, **Uhrichsville, Ohio**.

Chapter 9

What are the Odds?

After reading these stories in the first 8 chapters of this book, you have probably already formed an opinion on whether or not you believe me. Skeptics may find themselves brainstorming in an attempt to provide a reasonable explanation for my B.F. encounters. My reply simply would be, "Good luck!" I have spent the better part of my life trying to do the very same thing and have failed. The reasonable explanation (if you would simply believe it) is that these stories are real and cannot be explained away by natural logic or rationalization. However, hardcore skeptics won't stop until they find a way to belittle and falsify my claims of seeing the creature.

I fully understand that with writing a book such as this I am putting my reputation as a quote, "sane" person on the line. I stand in proxy for all others who have had similar experiences such as mine but were afraid to tell their stories for fear of public ridicule. Together we will take on the B.F. skeptics and not be moved just because we don't have "sufficient" enough evidence to back up our claims. I APOLOGIZE for the fact that Sasquatch didn't first make sure I had a camera before appearing to me and then we could have posed for "a selfie" together. Get real, man! This isn't *Harry and the Henderson's* we're talking about here, this is the REAL DEAL or the "Real McCoy."

In this chapter we are going to examine the incredible odds that the Bigfoot in my personal sightings and encounters may have been NOTHING MORE than some man dressed up in a monkey suit.

Once you see just how incredible and impractical the odds are of such a thing as this having occurred, **I think DOUBTERS will be turned into BELIEVERS after reading this**. At least, that's what I'm hoping for, anyway. At the very end of each example below, carefully consider what the odds would be that a man in a monkey suit was responsible for my encounters and then write them down when I ask. Please keep your odds at 10 to 1 of either the "entity" being a Bigfoot or a man. You will have 2 columns. The number on the left column will be how many points you assess or believe the entity to be a Bigfoot. And the number on your right column for it being a man. FYI, a "9" in either column is considered "irrefutable" evidence. For example, 8 to 2 is evidence of the entity being a Bigfoot, but because it's not a 9, it's not "irrefutable." Does everyone understand how to write down your odds? Ok, let's begin.

In chapter 1 of this book, you read where my friend George and I had to resituate our campsite on top of a high hill after nearly setting the area behind his barn on fire. This particular hill was at least, 200 feet or so in height. What made it even more difficult to access was all the sporadic briar bushes and thorn trees it was covered in which would easily prick you if you weren't careful. With that being said, how probable do you believe it would have been for some man dressed in a large, hot and hairy gorilla suit to have climbed this particular hill at 1 o'clock in the morning with *no flashlight*, just to scare a couple of kids out of their wits? And if so, how in the world did he know where to look for us at? Not even George's own family knew our exact whereabouts until we told them later, **AFTER** THE INCIDENT!

While this large hairy beast was standing a mere 5 feet away, I could easily tell it was much broader across the chest area than a normal human being, about 2 and a half times, at the very least. Combine that with its HEIGHT (8 ft.) AND WEIGHT (600 plus lbs.) and you have one **SUPER LARGE MONSTER** on your hands. How could someone have *possibly* faked being 8 foot tall, 2 and a half times broader than a regular man, hands hanging down to its knees, and weighing in at 600 lbs? Not to mention the fact, that the being had just run the 40 yard dash in approximately 3-4 seconds flat, a feat unheard of by today's standards or athletes (especially, weighing that much)! As the being ran away, I could easily tell this WAS THE REAL DEAL, folks! There was ***NO DOUBT IN MY MIND WHATSOEVER! THEN nor NOW!!!***

And what about the depth of the tracks (almost 2 inches deep)? How does that figure in if this is only some man trying to play tricks on a couple of young kids? How does a normal 200 pound man transform himself into a 600 lb. creature? Remember, John (George's dad) weighed 200 lbs and his track depth was about a half an inch. Simple multiplication would prove that 3 times a half an inch (with a ½ inch being 200 lbs.) would equal a 600 lb being, correct? And "*The Thing*" could have weighed much more than that because we're still a half inch shy! Even if we only give this guy an extra 400 lbs, a 200 lb man with an extra 400 lbs IS NOT GOING to sprint 40 yards in 3 or 4 seconds! To be quite honest, most men (myself included) can't even lift that much, much less carry it around with them while they run. Are you beginning to get the idea yet that something isn't adding up here, folks? You're not the only one, me, either.

Now, if that isn't enough to sink your "skeptic" battleship, try this one on for size! The next morning after we all had breakfast, we went up on top of the hill to see if we could find any tracks. We most certainly did and located about a dozen or so, all ranging anywhere from 7 to 9 feet between strides. The footprints themselves were approximately 15 inches long and about 7 inches wide (that's one big foot), but that wasn't the unbelievable part. The unbelievable part was located in the center of the logging road where the last track was found.

Where normally there should have been more footprints just up ahead, the tracks completely stopped for no apparent reason. Let me attempt to explain what I'm talking about using this particular analogy. Picture wet cement that's just been freshly laid where workers are making a new sidewalk. Now picture a dog that jumps onto the wet cement and walks right down through the middle of it. You can clearly see the dog's tracks, right? But what if someone reached down and picked up the dog from the sidewalk in order to preserve the rest of the job? The footprints would naturally stop right there, correct? Do you see what I mean?

In other words, something transpired on this particular spot that was **incomprehensible** for the natural mind to comprehend. What exactly happened? To be frank with you, I don't know. I have my theories, but at this point and juncture, that's all they really are. But one thing I do know, whatever happened, this being the locals called "Bigfoot" disappeared without a trace from this particular spot on the ground where the last track was found. And that, my friend, is **UNBELIEVABLE** or as I'd like to think, **"SUPERNATURAL!"** Surely, if this were just a 'flesh and blood' type of being, the footprints would have continued on across the logging road until they veered off to change direction. And then, it would only be natural to lose sight of the tracks, but not on smooth, level ground the same consistency. Do you see what I mean?

In order to conclude, all these things 'put together' point toward a creature of some sorts, not some man dressed in a monkey suit out playing tricks on a couple of young kids. The obstacles to overcome (given this particular set of circumstances) are UNBELIEVABLE! Let's review a few and you'll see what I mean.

1. A very steep hill of about 200 ft. to climb, all while wearing a huge, bulky gorilla suit that had to be very hot on a 75 degree night. Plus, this suit had to be extra tall (about 2 feet taller than an averaged size man) and extra wide (to account for the bulkiness I described earlier). It also had to have longer than normal arms to account for the hands hanging down to its knees. Shorter than normal legs and a longer than normal torso, plus a gorilla "cone head" that only reached about 10 inches above its shoulders because the rest of its face was tucked down into its chest. How many of you know "exactly" where you can purchase a Bigfoot suit like this? Let me break it down for you, there isn't any such place, ***especially*** back in 1972 when this particular event occurred. Now, today (05/2018), you CAN BUY a bigfoot suit, alright, but it's probably not going to look like the being I just described to you. Also, remember, this camping out "thing" was a spur of the moment decision on our part; it wasn't something "planned" way in advance. The decision was made on Friday to camp out and we camped out

that night. That's not much time to go purchase a B.F. suit, now is it?

2. Another interesting thing I remember is that when the creature hit the tent with his fist, he knew exactly where to punch. The tent in question was an old army tent, made up of dark green material which you COULD NOT see through (especially at night). How would *a person* know exactly where to punch at if he couldn't see through the material? We weren't making any noise and yet the being still hit us right on the head, both times! Either he was EXTREMELY LUCKY or he had *The Supernatural Ability* to see right through the material. Which do you think it was?

3. If this thing was merely some man dressed up in a monkey suit (with all the extra added attachments as I mentioned earlier), how could it have ran 40 yards in about 3 or 4 seconds? You may say, "How do you know it was just 3 or 4 seconds, were you timing it?" Of course, not. I mean, it may have been 5 seconds for all I know, but I seriously doubt it. The point is, this thing ran faster than any human I've ever witnessed in my life, and I'm talking about currently (May, 2018). And I'm sure if I dragged George into this story (I am respecting his right to privacy, of course) that he would agree with my analysis.

4. If the being who made those particular footprints was, indeed, 600 lbs as we believe, how did he run that fast being a regular sized man? Or an oversized one, for that matter? This question will probably end up stumping every single B.F. skeptic reading this book. How do I know? Simple, because it's literally "IMPOSSIBLE," naturally speaking! Do the math yourself and I bet you come up with the same conclusion as I did.

5. And last, but certainly, not least, where did the creature disappear to after its last known track in the center of the logging road? Enter the Twilight Zone, folks! With Rod Sterling as your host! Do, do, do, do, do, do, do, do, do, do, do, do, do, do...eerie music playing.

If you have plausible answers to all these questions and they make sense, I certainly want to talk to you because I've spent the last 40 years trying to figure it out and haven't been able to. Let me ask you a question. After reviewing the incredible things listed in the previous 5 points, did you happen to see anything that might be considered "quote" Supernatural in them? If you have to, go back and reread this material. I think if you do, you'll be amazed by what you find.

Now go ahead and write down your odds...(Are they 9 or greater to 1 in favor of the creature being a Bigfoot? Or just an ordinary man who pulled "off" an incredible stunt?) _____ to _____

Now let's go to the next and final story that we're going to cover here entitled, "*On the Trail of the Abominable Snowman*" as found in chapter 2.

With temps hovering in the mid-teens and a windchill factor of 5 to 10 degrees below zero, I set out hunting for a big buck during the last day of the 1972 deer shotgun season in Ohio. A couple of hours into my hunt I ran across several Bigfoot tracks in the snow. They weren't somebody's boot tracks or snowshoe tracks, that I can assure you of. They were compressed down into the white fluff about a couple of inches deeper than my own tracks with 3 big toes at the end, instead of the usual 5 in most other cases of these beings.

QUESTION. What are the odds of someone getting up out of bed between 4 and 5 o'clock in the morning (during the height of a snowstorm with winds gusting 25 mph or more) just to fool people into believing that a big hairy monster was somewhere nearby? Come on, now, really? Isn't it possible, you may very well ask? Of course, it's possible, but the better question might be, is it practical? Possible, yes, practical, no. Really, really no! At least I don't think so but you're the odd makers so it's entirely up to you.

My reason for being out there was simple, some good ole sweet venison and possibly, a trophy buck. But what would prompt a would-be prankster to get out of a nice warm bed during a howling snowstorm with temps in the teens and a windchill factor nearing 10 DEGREES BELOW ZERO just to lay down some B.F. tracks? Of which, I might add, most would probably get covered over by snow before anybody else even had a chance to see them? Not to mention the fact it was the very last day of the deer gun season, which means there would be idiots out there willing to shoot anything that moves, making it an *extremely* dangerous outing, to say the least. Are you beginning to see the ramifications yet of these Bigfoot prints belonging to a prankster? If not, I still have some more things to share with you and they keep on getting better and better the farther we go along.

As I began following the creature I've personally dubbed, **"THE ABOMINABLE SNOWMAN,"** I came to an old barb wire fence where apparently, it had crossed. However, the odd thing to me was that Sasquatch HAD NOT jumped over the fence as one might expect. He or it simply stepped over it and continued on walking. Granted, the fence wasn't very high, being only about 3 ½ to 4 feet, but still high enough that if a man wearing Bigfoot shoes would have crossed it, he would certainly have had to jump. Yet there was absolutely no indication whatsoever that the being who crossed over that fence had jumped. No splayed marks, no twisted feet as they would've landed, nothing but regular looking steps. I simply shook my head in amazement as I continued following the tracks, but my biggest astonishment lay just ahead of me yet to discover.

After following the tracks for just a short distance past the fence and slightly up a hill, I discovered where they led into a small cave in what appeared to be a large mound. The cave entrance itself was small, perhaps measuring no more than 3 feet wide and about the same in height. There were also briar branches dangling over the top of it with snow clearly attached to them, making me wonder how in the world a 7 to 8 foot tall creature could have entered that cave WITHOUT first knocking off the snow on those briars. For a brief moment I stood there contemplating that very question, but all I could deduct from current observations was that the creature had to be in there somewhere because no other tracks were seen leading out of the cave. And I wasn't about to get down on my hands and knees and end up crawling into a place where Mr. Bigfoot might be curled up sleeping at. Forget that one, Jack!

If you've been following the story closely, you must by now realize the tremendous odds against this creature simply being some man wearing a pair of Bigfoot sneakers. In fact, in my opinion, it would be downright **impossible** for this thing (whatever it was) to be a prankster just out for a morning stroll in a snowstorm to fool people. Here is a brief list of things to consider before writing down your odds.

1. The weather conditions were simply downright brutally cold and nasty, to say the very least.
2. It was the last day of the deer shotgun season. Anyone out there hunting would probably be willing to shoot at anything that moves. This would make a prankster's foolish endeavor even more dangerous than perhaps the weather itself.
3. The creature simply STEPPED over a 4 foot fence rather than jumping it. I think we all know not many men on the face of this earth would have the capability to do that, especially wearing a pair of B.F. shoes on their feet.
4. The B.F. tracks clearly led into a small cave with NO OTHER tracks seen anywhere around the earthen mound they went into. Clearly, whatever or whoever had made those tracks was still inside that cave somewhere. If true, this would completely rule out the possibility that a man was laying in there trying to get some sleep when the temperature was so dangerously cold outside. In fact, it has been proven before that in those type of conditions, frostbite is imminent if one is exposed to the elements for very long. Obviously, if this was a REAL MAN he definitely wouldn't have been laying in a cave somewhere playing Bigfoot during those type of conditions, correct? I think we can all agree upon that one, at the very least.
5. The being whose tracks I followed that day KNEW EXACTLY where he or it was going! That means they had obviously been there before, correct? Either a man with Bigfoot shoes knew that place intimately and had accessed that cave several times before

OR an unknown primate, cryptid or monster had been using it on a regular basis as a bedding spot or even a home, if you please. Which do you think it was? To me, it's a NO BRAINER!

My observations that day lead me to believe that I probably ran across a Bigfoot creature **"out on the prowl"** that night. Then, upon seeing how harsh the conditions were getting headed back to his warm, dry bed to get some much needed comfort and rest. Nevertheless, those are just my observations and conclusions; the choice is ultimately, up to you. In other words, what are the odds, given these set of circumstances, that this particular entity was ONLY a man wearing B.F. sneakers out on a morning stroll through the woods?

Please go ahead now and write down your odds. _____ to _____

Most people (even hardened skeptics, I believe)) would easily deduct that I quite possibly did run across a GENUINE set of Bigfoot tracks in the snow that last day of the 1972 deer shotgun season in Ohio. If that is your conclusion, then congratulations, you have passed the test of a normal thinking person putting aside all preconceived notions in order to reasonably assess a given situation without being bias. I applaud you! To the rest of you, I can only assume that you probably don't believe my story to begin with. Am I correct? I bet you that I am because that's the only way one COULD NOT COME to the conclusion that this WAS some type of a Bigfoot being. *To me, the signs are so obvious they're as plain as the nose is on your face!*

We could continue playing this little game and I could help you conclude that each one of my stories have absolutely **"astounding odds"** against being fake or that someone went to a heck of a lot of trouble just to scare the living daylights out of me. However, the points would be more repetitive and redundant, therefore, I digress. Hopefully, everyone understands what I'm trying to convey here. Stay tuned for the next exciting chapter where we discuss the CURRENT EVIDENCE for Sasquatch verses the FAKE EVIDENCE! And believe it or not, THERE IS A DIFFERENCE between the two as you'll eventually find out.

Chapter 10

Prosecuting Bigfoot: Where's the Evidence?

O ver the years thousands of people have reported seeing a large bipedal, hairy looking creature called Sasquatch (aka Bigfoot). However, scientists and skeptics alike want to know where all the evidence is at to support such outlandish claims? Their question exists for a valid reason. To date, no one has ever found an actual body or bones of one of these "supposed" type of beings before (contemporary or fossilized). In comparison, fossils are still being found of extinct creatures such as dinosaurs and wooly mammoths which disappeared from earth eons ago. So where's Bigfoot at, they naturally ask? With nothing concrete such as a body or bones to examine, the scientific community is left with no other choice than to dismiss the possibility that the creature exists.

To date, the strongest piece of evidence supporting that Bigfoot is real happens to be a short, rather *shaky piece* of video footage called the "Patterson-Gimly film," taken from the Bluff Creek area of Northern California in 1967. More on this film in a little bit.

You would think, however, that with the passage of time since then and all of our modern day technology, something else would have surfaced by now that would have provided additional proof of the creature's existence? Yes, I would most certainly agree with that assumption. However, before outright dismissing hundreds of "credible" FIRST-HAND eyewitness accounts of Sasquatch because of this, let's first examine the majority of evidence we do have. For example, if we were to take Bigfoot to a Court of Law, would we have enough "circumstantial evidence" to prosecute him for living among us? Let's see if we can add some clarity to this rather ominous question. The answer may determine whether the bizarre creature actually exists or not.

In the following examples I will list the "quote" circumstantial evidence of Bigfoot and then, like a lawyer, examine its credibility. I will then list a number from 1 to 10 that based upon "my" personal opinion, lends credence to the creature's existence. The closer to 10, the more likely it is to be considered "credible" or "authentic" evidence.

1. The immense number of **<u>EYE WITNESS ACCOUNTS</u>** spread over the many centuries, including Native Americans who were the original inhabitants of our N.A. continent.

As you probably know, not many people put a lot of stock or credibility into eyewitness accounts. The reason? They can and have been wrong or purposely manipulated before. For example, just because you may have seen someone at a certain place and time where an actual crime or murder was committed DOES NOT necessarily prove that that person was the one who did it. Wouldn't they be considered "suspect," you may ask? Of course, they would, but the entire course of action has to be determined or proved "beyond the shadow of a doubt" before the judge or jury will find them guilty of the crime.

If someone has been seen at the time and place of a crime, the defendant's lawyer will then ask a series of questions to the eyewitness in order to determine their credibility. For example, what is the eyewitness's occupation? Other questions may include the following. What time of day did the incident or crime occur? What was the weather like? Where were they when they seen the defendant? What were they doing there? Did they see anyone else in the immediate vicinity who may have possibly been involved, etc. and etc.

In the case of an eyewitness claiming to have seen a large hairy monster, the entire story needs to be reiterated in order to obtain more information concerning the event. Not including other factors previously mentioned, all these things need to be considered in regards to the eye witness's credibility. If everything checks out O.K., then it's relatively certain we can take the eyewitness's word for their testimony, report, story, etc.. However, if something seems amiss, the judge will dismiss the person's testimony and throw it out. The last thing anybody wants is for the wrong person to get convicted of a crime they didn't commit. The same principle applies toward someone claiming to have seen a Sasquatch, as well, except there's no criminal intent involved here, just perhaps a case of mistaken identity or someone playing a bad practical joke. Nevertheless, we are ultimately after the truth herein and WILL NOT accept ANYTHING LESS!

With that last thought in mind, how probable would it be that literally hundreds of super "credible" witnesses from all over the world would be lying about their encounters with a creature resembling Bigfoot or Sasquatch? In most cases we are talking about VERY HONORABLE CITIZENS, including certain policemen, doctors, lawyers, nurses, airline pilots, businessmen, pastors, teachers, government officials, etc. and etc. Even one President of the United States, Teddy Roosevelt, has reportedly believed that an upright, tall hairy humanoid being was seen walking around in the forests and woodlands of his day as reported to him by one of his very close friends. It has been rumored before by those who knew President Theodore Roosevelt the best, that he went to his grave believing in the existence of Sasquatch.

And what about Native American accounts of seeing the Big Hairy Man (aka Sasquatch)? I know, not many people may be inclined to believe in the Indian's reports, right? But why not? Is it because they just don't like Indians or don't believe they're very credible? Let me remind you that in a Court of Law, you have to put aside your personal feelings when discussing a case or you may be dismissed from it for being biased.

Our Native American friends are people like you and I and need to be taken seriously for their claims just like anyone else. They, too, (especially being the first inhabitants of this land,) have seen the big hairy creature before and the tracks it has left behind as proof of its existence. Several stories of Sasquatch have been told in their oral legends dating back thousands of years. There are also Stone Paintings called ***petroglyphs*** that show Native Americans interacting with what appears to be a Bigfoot-like creature right here on our North American continent (in the State of Georgia). Which prompts the ominous question, "Could the Native American Legend of Bigfoot really be true?" Or are all these sighting reports (including the white man's) just cases of mistaken identity or other fabricated claims for different purposes?

Even if we throw out 95 % of all eyewitness reports as hoaxes or mistaken cases of identity, we still have 5 % that defy natural logic and therefore, simply cannot be explained. In other words (as ominous as it may sound), SOMETHING IS OUT THERE scaring the heck out of people and as intelligent as we claim to be, we simply have no clue as to what it actually is.

Consider this story by Nyna Heury, a cab driver from Alaska, taken from the back cover of the book by *Animal Planet* entitled, *Finding Bigfoot: Everything You Need To Know."*

Ft. #1

"Nyna Henry drives a cab on Alaska's Prince of Whale's Island, making regular trips back and forth during the night. On one of those wee-hours trips, she had a passenger with her.

"Out of nowhere, this piece of wood comes flying at us, she said. "It hit the front end of the car and cracked my windshield all the way across."

Something big had to have thrown it because the impact shook her entire van. Nyna wanted to stop, but her frightened passenger urged her on. She returned to investigate the next day and found the piece of wood. It smelled putrid. She looked up into a nearby tree and saw a big pair of green eyes looking at her from inside a "humongous" body.

"There's no way it was a bear," she said.

"It's a strange story," Bobo Fay said, "but sasquatches are strange animals. They do weird things." 1

Because we don't believe in Bigfoot, are we justified in dismissing Nyna's story as an outright lie or simply claim that she's delusional?

This woman saw something when she returned to the site that defies normal descriptions of natural animals, plus a big pair of green eyes, to boot! Is this something normal? Of course, not. And neither are Bigfoot sightings, in general, BUT I BELIEVE THEY ARE REAL NONETHELESS. Besides, HUNDREDS OF PEOPLE ALL OVER THIS WORLD SIMPLY **"CANNOT"** BE ALL WRONG!!!

On a Sasquatch Sighting map from Joshua Steven's website called:

Ft. #2 *Squatch Watch: 92 Years of Bigfoot Sightings in the US and Canada,* printed on September 17, 2013, F.2 we find the following information listed.

On this particular map, the State of Ohio is shown with SEVERAL Sasquatch sightings. And the exact area in which I USED TO LIVE IN (Tuscarawas County) is labeled with little purple blocks (meaning... Sasquatch sightings GALORE). And I never reported my sightings!

My question is, "If I never reported mine and other people never reported theirs for fear of public ridicule, how many sightings per "actual reported sightings" do you think there really are?" 3, 5, 10 or more? I don't know, but I'm guessing there's at least 3 (minimal, that is). If so, we don't have a Bigfoot/Sasquatch problem, my friend, we have A BIGFOOT/SASQUATCH…… INFESTATION!!!

In light of all the preceding information on actual sightings reported, I only give SIGHTINGS about a 5 on my scale of credibility. In other words, I believe that 5 people out of 10 REPORTED SIGHTINGS actually saw something they can't explain. Perhaps 2 of the last 5 "thought they saw a Sasquatch" but really weren't sure. The other 3 may have only reported something because they wanted to tell an outlandish story to either fool somebody or to gain unwarranted attention, not sure exactly which.

2. <u>The Creature's Footprints!</u>

Famous for his name, Sasquatch, the elusive cryptid, isn't called "Bigfoot" for nothing. Over the last 50 years there have been approximately 900 to a 1,000 casts supposedly made of the creature's footprints. Most of these average 15 to 18 inches long and 7 inches wide. By comparison, one 7'3" basketball player (an abnormality himself) has a foot measuring 16 ½ inches long and 5 ½ inches wide. So the average Bigfoot has him beat by a couple of extra inches in width. You have to admit, that's ONE BIG FOOT!

However, like eyewitness accounts, B.F. tracks can also easily be faked. With that said, of the 1,000 B.F. print casts in existence, I'm guessing that the majority of them are actually fake. Notice, I didn't say ALL, just a majority. If I were to guess, I'd put the number around 700 or so. Wow, you're probably thinking, that's an awful lot for a die-hard B.F. believer like you to admit. And you're absolutely right! However, I'm only being realistic in my analysis. You see, I've done my homework. I've read several of the skeptic reports on the internet and confess, a lot of them have made some valid points which I have reiterated from time to time in this book. However, not all of their points are true and factual as they claim. I have noticed, through lots of time honored research, a lot of educated guesses and "supposed" conclusions based upon their negative views of B.F., and that's ultimately where they go wrong in their otherwise, well written articles.

With the above being said, let's ASSUME for the moment that 850 B.F. cast prints are actually fake. I don't personally believe there are THAT MANY, but let's give them the benefit of a doubt. That would still leave 100 to 150 prints in which there are no plausible reasons for the tracks being where they were found. For example, who is going to hike more than 5 miles through absolute briars, brambles, and thorn trees...up over mountain ranges, down into remote valleys and across raging rivers in order to put down 2 to 3 fake B.F. tracks and then walk another 5 miles back out through the same conditions? Not too many people, correct? Are you beginning to get my point? And that's exactly where some of these B.F. casts were made. That particular information throws a whole new light on the subject, now doesn't it?

Although I hate to admit this, even "quote" experts in the field of anthropology have reportedly been duped before when it comes to authenticating "REAL" B.F. tracks from "fake" ones. Dr. Grover Krantz (an anthropologist from Washington State University) was once given what he believed to be a genuine set of B.F. prints based upon anatomical features of what appeared to be an injured primate foot. However, Michael Dennett, an investigator for the *Skeptical Inquirer*, tracked down the anonymous construction worker who supplied the Bigfoot print. The man admitted to Dennett that he had, indeed, made the track himself and gave it to Dr. Krantz to see if he could tell the difference or not. Apparently, according to the *Skeptical Inquirer*, he couldn't.

On the other hand, there are, believe it or not, actual "REAL" B.F. tracks out there and have been found in recent years. For example, Richard Noll, a wildlife tracker, found several B.F. tracks near Skookum Meadows, Big Creek, Washington State on October the 20th, 2002. He took 2 photos of these which are available to see on the BFRO website. The report # is 5176 (www.bfro.net). As a matter of fact, these particular B.F. prints actually led to the discovery of what has been called, "The Skookum Body cast" or what many believe to be a partial body imprint of a real Sasquatch. Details of this find will be forthcoming in the next section.

In 1982, Sheriff deputy, Dennis Heryford, made 5 plaster cast molds of a 15 " alleged Sasquatch print found in Washington State. It measured 2 inches deep and 6 inches wide and showed similar features everyone would expect to find in a real B.F. track. These included toenails, tendons, dermal ridges and bunions. In fact, several of these 15 inch tracks were found in clusters by more than one person and to top it off, hair samples were also found with these prints, as well; which deputy Heryford sent to a laboratory for analysis. Of these, one was found to be human, but another had a "non-human root," and DID NOT resemble any known human or primate hairs on record.

As might be expected, people who have seen and studied these tracks believe they are the REAL DEAL. Those who HAVE NOT seen them often dismiss them as being fraudulent and the work of hoaxers. Several of these people have recently been featured in newspaper articles holding up their crudely carved B.F. prints of which they claimed to have made tracks with before. Obviously, this does little to bolster belief in the creature whom many claim to have seen throughout North America in the last 50 years.

However, not all Bigfoot tracks appear to have been made by a mold. Many show what appear to be a foot IN MOTION. Toes are in different positions in the wet soil. Heel imprints are at different depths, signifying different weight distributions of the animal. A partial imprint may indicate the Bigfoot was also running. A few tracks even show details of skin texture called ***dermatoglyphs*** (fingerprint like marks) found on the bottom of the foot, as well. This particular feature is nearly impossible to fake by a prankster using *pre-carved* molds as templates. Any particular B.F. prints with *dermatoglyphs* found on the soul of the foot are, I believe, the work of a real-life Sasquatch, not a prankster's creativity.

The Elkins Creek Cast

One can hardly talk about *dermatoglyphs* (also called "dermal ridges") without bringing up the subject of the "Elkins Creek Cast." This print was discovered by Deputy James P. Atkin in 1994 as he was investigating an elderly man's complaints that someone was terrorizing his home in Pike County, Georgia, close to Elkins Creek. The disturbances first started off by a constant rapping noise on the man's house and progressed to forcible pounding and several missing items, like sacks of dog food and corn. At first, Deputy Atkin surmised that because of its secluded location, the disturbances may have been the work of moonshiners or marijuana growers trying to scare the old man and woman off their property. This way, he thought, they could have the entire area to themselves to carry out their illegal shenanigans. But every attempt to catch the perpetrators had come up empty handed. The entire Police force was beginning to think that the old man and his wife were simply making these stories up.

One night the man called in and reported that the door to his shed had been completely ripped off of its hinges and more items had come up missing. Having battled these nightly raids now for more than six months, he demanded answers. Once again, Deputy Atkin was dispatched to the scene and not being able to find anything that night, asked the man if he could come back during the day to investigate things more thoroughly. The man agreed and the next day proved to be a more fruitful investigation.

As the Deputy was checking around the property he noticed a huge tractor tire had apparently been thrown 30 feet high into a nearby tree. This find started him thinking that these nightly excursions may be something more than the work of a few vandals. Whoever had thrown that tire into the tree must have possessed superhuman strength. He recalled talking to a man earlier who had reported seeing a large hairy beast run across the road on two feet just a short distance away from the man's property. Could there be a connection, he wondered? Fortunately, he wouldn't have to wait long to find out.

After investigating the area close to the man's house, Deputy Atkin decided to follow a game trail that led down toward Elkins Creek. He was trying to find a path that might have been used by the intruder in order to set up an ambush later on. As he neared the creek he began having an eerie feeling that he was being watched, so he put his hand on his gun and kept a close eye out on his surroundings. Once he approached the creek he began walking along the edge until he spotted what appeared to be 'tracks' on the muddy bank. As he stepped down to have a closer look, the Deputy struck paydirt, "literally." There laying before him was a huge footprint (measuring 17.5 inches long and 8.5 inches wide), plus he could also make out 4 other tracks of the same size in the creek, as well. Realizing this was a monumental find to his investigation, he returned to his truck to get some plaster paris to make a cast of the print.

To make a long story short, this particular B.F. cast was sent off to Dr. Grover Krantz of Washington State University, who, after studying it, believed it to be an authentic cast of an unknown North American primate. Dr. Krantz then shared the cast with Jeff Meldrum, professor of anatomy and anthropology at Idaho State University, and Jimmy Chilcutt, former Latent Fingerprint Examiner for the Conroe Police Department in Texas. Both Meldrum and Chilcutt conducted a detailed analysis of the track and found evidence of primate-like **dermal ridges** and even **sweat pores** that showed up under magnification. According to Chilcutt (an expert in the area of human and primate identification), he concluded, based upon his findings, that the "Elkins Creek Cast" was the "real deal" and belonged to an UNKNOWN PRIMATE.

So, there, we have just discussed both "fake" and "real" examples of Bigfoot prints. It should be noted that there are several hundreds of photos of alleged B.F. prints on the internet (most, I assume, are probably fake). However, I chose Wildlife Tracker Richard Noll's B.F. prints as "real," in my opinion, because he is a certified member the BFRO (Bigfoot Research Organization), a professional group of men whom I highly doubt would ever intentionally fake evidence of the creature. I also included Sheriff deputy Dennis Heryford's 15 inch track cast as real because of the different positions of the toes, bunions and heels, plus the clear and unusual design of the *dermatoglyphs* found on the bottom of the footprints. In addition to all of that, hair samples were also found with these tracks, as well. This would seem to make the find even more relevant OR should I "dare" say "VALID?"

And what can you say about the "Elkins Creek Cast?" The actual story behind this find sounds like something straight out of a horror movie, but is one hundred percent true, nonetheless. Not mentioned in the prelude, the man's dogs (over a period of about 6 months) began disappearing one by one, plus their food, as well. Even more bizarre, the man claimed that on a few occasions, he and his wife could hear someone **trying to speak** to them from outside their house in *a very crude* (rough or hoarse) *voice*; which, of course, they couldn't comprehend. The entire story can be found in Lyle Blackburn's book entitled *"BEYOND BOGGY CREEK: In Search of the Southern Sasquatch."* This is one of the best collection of Bigfoot stories ever assembled, I believe, a "must have" if you're a true Bigfooter. The "Elkins Creek Cast" is considered by many different experts to be one of the best examples of an "authentic" unknown primate's footprint on record. And it was found upon the banks of Elkins Creek, right here in the State of Georgia. Remember, folks, THEY... ALWAYS... FOLLOW...THE CREEKS!

Even with these "alleged" REAL TRACKS, I'm only going to give the B.F. prints about a 6 on my scale of "credible evidence" in proving Bigfoot's existence. I would go a little bit higher, but I'm afraid there are way too many "fake" prints out there to justifiably do so. Remember, just because someone shows you a B.F. print doesn't necessarily mean it came from a genuine Sasquatch, so be careful while assessing the footprint and the person supplying it. Also, don't forget to ask a lot of questions to ensure credibility before buying their story or their print!

3. <u>The Skookum Body Cast!</u>

Probably ranking as the No.2 piece of purported Bigfoot evidence next to the "Patterson-Gimly film," is the "Skookum body cast." It is believed to have been made by an adult male Bigfoot in the Skookum Meadows area of the Gifford Pinchot National Forest in Washington State. The cast measures 3.5 by 5 feet and weighs approximately 400 pounds. It appears to be, according to the BFRO who conducted the initial examination, THE IMPRINT OF A LARGE ANIMAL'S LEFT FOREARM, HIP, THIGH, and HEEL.

Matt Moneymaker and other members of the Bigfoot Research Organization (BFRO) team made the initial discovery as they were checking fruit traps baited with melons, apples and peanuts. At 9 o'clock in the morning on September the 22nd, 2000, three of the team members noticed fruit missing from one of the sites, surrounded by several tracks of different animals. Upon examination of the area they happened to notice an unusual impression at the edge of a muddy wallow. Members of the team discussed the impression left in the mud and concluded that this "may be" <u>THE VERY FIRST</u> **BODY PRINT** of **A REAL SASQUATCH** (Bigfoot). The base camp of researchers were alerted and everyone went over to check the site out.

A discussion ensued as to why the animal or Sasquatch didn't just walk up to the bait and take it as most other animals normally would have? One possible explanation, a few noted, was that because this was a high traffic area, the purported beast DID NOT want to leave behind obvious signs of its presence. The team noted that according to the imprint, the creature had apparently sat down and reached over to the bait (putting weight on its left forearm) so it wouldn't leave any tracks. Some researchers said that during investigations of other Sasquatch sightings, they, too, had noticed this type of phenomenon before. One researcher commented that if these animals have been avoiding confrontations with humans for thousands of years, then this type of behavior would only be considered normal. In other words, they would naturally make special efforts to reduce their sign to as minimal as possible. As confirmation, most "genuine tracks" have been more commonly observed in remote areas, such as the Bluff Creek area in Northern California in 1967 (the Patterson-Gimly film), as an example.

Apple cores, along with several other chewed up pieces of apple were also found laying near the imprint. Members of the BFRO team mentioned that if this animal would simply have been an elk, deer, or coyote, it probably would have eaten the entire apple. FYI, apes DO NOT normally eat the core of an apple, thus this seemingly minor detail may, in fact, become a major one while trying to assess what type of animal made the Skookum impression in the mud.

Other important and relative details were noted, as well. For more information on these, please go to the BFRO website: www.BFRO.net .

Once back at the lab, a special team of investigators were called in to assess the important find. The investigative team included Dr. Jeff Meldrum (associate professor of anatomy and anthropology at Idaho State University); Dr. Grover Krantz (retired physical anthropologist from Washington State University); Dr. John Bindernagel (Canadian Wildlife biologist); John Green (retired Canadian journalist and author); and Dr. Ron Brown (exotic animal handler and healthcare administrator). After careful examination, this team of professional scientists and researchers concluded that this particular imprint COULD NOT have been made by any commonly known Northwest animal and MAY REPRESENT an unknown primate. My thoughts when I read this, Bigfoot, perhaps?

Other Sasquatch evidence found at the site by the BFRO expedition included voice recordings and indistinct, blurry impressions of 17 inch footprints. Preliminary measurements of the impression indicate that its body dimensions are 40 to 50 percent LARGER than that of a six foot tall human being. Another feature of the Skookum cast which is highly relevant in pointing to a Bigfoot has to do with one particular hair strand found on it. A footnote from the BFRO expedition website says:

Ft. #3

"Hair samples collected at the scene and from the cast itself and examined by Dr. Henner Fahrenbach, a biomedical research scientist from Beaverton, Ore., were primarily of deer, elk, coyote, and bear as was expected since tracks in the wallow were mostly of those animals.

However, based on characteristics matching those of otherwise indeterminate primate hairs collected in association with other Sasquatch sightings, he identified a single distinctly primate hair as "Sasquatch." 3

Based upon the expertise of these top-notch researchers and experts, Idaho State University issued a press release about the find, quoting Dr. Jeff Meldrum:

Ft. #4

"While not definitely proving the existence of a species of North American ape, the cast constitutes significant and compelling new evidence that will hopefully stimulate further serious research and investigation into the presence of these primates in the Northwest mountains and elsewhere." 4

Skeptics, though, counteract that the initial observation by Richard Noll (one of the BFRO team members involved in the initial find) may have greatly influenced the rest of the team to PREMATURELY agree with his analysis before they had a chance to study the impression themselves. This may or may not be true, we simply don't know for absolutely certain. However, other professionals WHO **WERE NOT THERE** during the initial discovery and still, after much prolonged evaluation of the cast, ended up validating the BFRO's team's original analysis. In other words, a team of top experts in their fields of expertise concluded that this find MAY BE "actual evidence" of an unknown North American primate. That's a very BIG STATEMENT, folks!

Dr. Jeff Meldrum later wrote a book in 2006 entitled, "*Sasquatch: Legend Meets Science.*" In it, the doctor discussed the analysis of the Skookum cast and described the findings of the group of scientists who examined it by saying:

Ft. 5

"The unanimous consensus was that this could very well be a body imprint of a Sasquatch." 5

Another doctor who later examined the Skookum cast was Dr. Daris Swindler, a retired professional of anatomy from the university of Washington. Originally, Dr. Swindler had been skeptical of the existence of Bigfoot, but after viewing the Skookum 400 lb. chunk of plaster he became convinced of the probable existence of a bipedal North American ape.

Some professionals have gone on record as endorsing the cast as solid proof of the existence of Sasquatch. Others believe the imprint is more conclusive to being that of the hindquarters of an elk (because elk hairs and prints were observed on the cast.) So, in essence, the jury is still out on this particular piece of "alleged" Bigfoot evidence. Irregardless of the jury, based upon statements by professionals in their field of expertise, I'm going to give the Skookum Cast an "8" on my Scale of "credible B.F. evidence." In other words, it rates what I would refer to as high, but not high enough to be "quote" irrefutable. In my opinion, the Skookum cast rates a very close "second place" next to the "Patterson-Gimly film" which will be discussed next.

4. <u>**Video Photographic Evidence of the Creature!**</u>

Nearly everyone who has ever looked into or studied the B.F. phenomenon has either seen or heard about the "Patterson-Gimly film" shot in a remote area of Northern California in 1967. Roger Patterson (a rodeo rider from Yakima, Washington) decided he would try to make a documentary about the Bigfoot mystery after having heard about numerous tracks spotted in the Bluff Creek area. As the story goes, a moment before Patterson spotted the creature his horse became startled and Roger nearly fell off of it. However, after seeing what startled his horse, Roger wasted no time in grabbing his camera and began shooting video footage of an "ALLEGED" Bigfoot walking across a dry creek bed until it disappeared out of sight. To date, many are calling this tape "irrefutable" evidence of the creature's existence. But is it? Whatever it is, it has stood the test of time because today, over 50 years later, NO ONE has yet been able to prove 'beyond the shadow of a doubt' that the film is a forgery.

However, a weak link in the story stems from various men having come forward claiming to have been THE MAN in THE MONKEY SUIT. However, there are several problems with their stories. For starters, if it was a man there could only be ONE MAN, not 3 or 4, I think we can all agree upon that one, right? Number 2, their stories all conflict with one another and Number 3 (and perhaps, most importantly), not one of them have ever been able to produce the amazing gorilla suit allegedly worn that afternoon in 1967. Don't you find these particular facts alone, suspicious, to say the least? Red flags, anybody?

According to www.animalplanet.com, they say:

F. #6

"No one has ever brought forward the actual costume involved, and no one has ever been able to create a matching costume, though many have tried." 6

To me, this is the single greatest proof that the Patterson-Gimly film is **The REAL DEAL** because of the TOTAL ABSENCE of the *particular suit* in question that was "supposedly" worn during the actual filming in 1967. In other words, it's really quite simple, folks: NO SUIT...**REAL BIGFOOT!** A REAL, ACTUAL SUIT...**FAKE BIGFOOT!** It doesn't get any more plain or simple than that, now does it? It seems quite clear that **THE CHALLENGE** has been issued!

In plain simple words, *__"Either produce THE ORIGINAL SUIT or KEEP QUIET about the ALLEGED Bigfoot being some man dressed up in a Monkey Suit!"__*

There are also OTHER anatomical problems involved with making a matching costume that resembled the 1967 version, as well. The animal-planet website elaborates:

Ft. #7

"The difficulty in creating a matching costume has to do with Limb ratios. The figure in the footage has shorter legs and longer arms, proportionally, than a human. The differences are most apparent when the figure is juxtaposed to the figure of a human in a bigfoot costume." 7

Skeptics, though, still abound.

F. #8

"Several Hollywood Insiders, including *"An American werewolf in London"* director John Landis, have claimed that the film shows a man dressed in an ape suit. According to Landis, the suit was designed by John Chambers, the special effects master who created costumes for the original *"Planet of the Apes"* movies. Chambers denies any involvement, but the rumor persists." 8

Believers also point out that a key piece of evidence of the film's credibility is how the creature walks. When humans walk, they lock their knees with each step, holding their legs straight. When the figure in the film walks, it keeps its knees bent the whole time it's walking, a striking difference. It is nearly impossible for a human being to walk that way because his or her body simply will not allow it, even if they try to duplicate the style.

Another remarkable characteristic differing from a man in a gorilla suit is how the skin and fur has a rippling motion, wherein the viewer can detect certain muscle groups on the creature's body. Supposing that the figure in the film weighs in excess of 500 lbs, this is exactly what one would expect to see if it was a real being. However, skeptics are quick to counter that the same rippling-skin effect can be obtained by attaching a "water-bag" under the suit.

Ft. #9

"According to E! On Line: *Bigfoot Movie: A Hollywood Hoax?*, several Hollywood effect artists say the figure is obviously a guy in an ape suit with a water-bag fastened to his stomach."9

However, one expert disagrees. According to Bill Munns (Bigfoot Researcher/Graphic Artist/Computer Animator and Hollywood Costume Designer) and the only man alive who has actually viewed the original "Patterson-Gimly film" shot in 1967, the controversial figure walking across the dry creek bed in Bluff Creek, California WAS NOT a man dressed in a gorilla suit, but a REAL LIFE, LIVING BREATHING PRIMATE of UNKNOWN ORIGINS.

CONCLUSION: In light of everything that's been said about this controversial film, I give it a "9" on my scale of Credibility. In other words, I personally believe the "Patterson-Gimly film" is the REAL DEAL. According to my research, I read where one very knowledgeable man in particular who interviewed Roger Patterson and Bob Gimly, concluded from his observations that neither one of these men were smart enough to pull off a prank of this magnitude (especially one that has endured for more than 50 years). Therefore, in his opinion, he believed that these 'happy go lucky' guys actually did run across a REAL Bigfoot that October afternoon in 1967.

5. <u>Native American and Indian Tribes Oral Traditions and Legends going back hundreds of years.</u>

It is no secret that Native American Indian tribes have stories describing GIANT HAIRY CREATURES in their oral traditions which date back several centuries. These particular stories sound eerily similar to the creature we know of today called Sasquatch or Bigfoot.

Many of these tribes have different languages or variants of the native tongue, suggesting these accounts DID NOT originate in the same place. Plus, each tribe has their own name for the creature, whom they regard as a sacred being. From the website entitled: http://www.bfro.net/legends/ we read:

Ft.#10

"Here in the Northwest, and west of the Rockies generally, Indian people regard Bigfoot with great respect. He is seen as a special kind of being, because of his obvious close relationship with humans. Some elders regard him as standing on the "border" between animal-style consciousness and human-style consciousness, which gives him a special kind of power." 10

They also regard the entity as a Special kind of Messenger. The same website continues:

Ft. # 11

"Ralph Graywolf, a visiting Athapaskan Indian from Alaska, told the reporter, "In our way of beliefs, they make appearances at troubled times" to help troubled Indian communities "get more in tune with Mother Earth." Bigfoot brings "signs or messages that there is a need to change, a need to cleanse." (Minn. news article, *"Giant Footprints Signals a Time to Seek Change."* July 23, 1988) 11

Continuing with the theme of Bigfoot being a Special Kind of Messenger, the Hopi Indian elders say that the increasing number of Bigfoot/Sasquatch sightings are not only a warning to particular individuals, but mankind at large. They see the creature as a Messenger who appears in evil times as a warning from the Creator that humanity, as a whole, has disrespected His sacred instructions, which, in turn, has upset the harmony and balance of existence. And these same elders warn that the more frequent the Big Man appears to people, the closer to the End of Days we are getting. Throughout Native North America the existence of Sasquatch/Bigfoot is taken for granted. They don't doubt the creature's existence whatsoever!

Ft. 12

"In Indian culture, the entire natural world - the animals, the plants, the rivers, the stars - IS SEEN AS FAMILY. And Bigfoot is seen as one of our close relatives, the "great elder brother." 12

Conclusion: Knowing it is a historical fact that the Indians were here before us, it is NOT SURPRISING to hear that they have such a close relationship with the creature we know of as Bigfoot/Sasquatch. And who am I or anyone else for that matter, to doubt their oral traditions and legends about the "Big Man," another synonym the Indians use for Sasquatch?

Therefore, I am going to give the Native American traditions and legends a whopping "9" on my Credibility scale of trustworthiness. Remember, this is MY SCALE or perspective, not anyone else's or organization's.

6. <u>Recordings of Bigfoot/Sasquatch!</u>

Now you're really stretching the pendulum, you're probably thinking. Are you really serious, here? Yes, I most certainly am. There are several types of noises or sounds that Sasquatch is said to have made before. Probably the most common one is the lone "howl," which usually lasts anywhere from 10 to 15 seconds or more, depending on the creature. Speaking from personal experience, it is a rather chilling sound that seems to go right through one's self, especially if you're in close proximity. Another comment concerning the "howl" of a Sasquatch that I like is found on *"The Legend of Bigfoot - Native American Legend Sasquatch"* website. It says:

Ft. # 13

"Not many of us have detected the lonely, chilling cries and howls of

Sasquatch. However, those that have, and recognize the sounds of the forest; say its an unforgettable sound like no other." 13

Being on the receiving end of these type of calls, not once, but twice in my life, I can vouch for the validity of this Indian statement! I know that I personally WILL NEVER, EVER FORGET either one of those times that I heard the cries...**NEVER EVER!!!**

Other sounds Sasquatch's like to make are "Wood knocking" noises. Usually associated as a means of communicating with one another, a lonely Sasquatch will pick up a piece of wood and slam it against a tree trunk in order to create a sound that has far reaching effects. If successful, the lone primate will hear another resounding knock from another of its kind. This is a very popular and often successful tactic used by Bigfoot researchers anywhere where there have been multiple B.F. sightings reported.

Sasquatch creatures, especially in family groupings, have also been heard making noises and sounds reminiscent of humans talking to one another. It's like they have an oral communication or language similar to human beings, except theirs is totally different. Perhaps the most compelling collection of recordings ever made are referred to as the *"Sierra Sounds,"* produced by Ron Morehead and taken from California's *Sierra Nevada Mountains* in the 1970's. Ron has been investigating the Bigfoot/Sasquatch phenomenon for decades and is a well known speaker at conferences. His collection of Bigfoot sound recordings are the only ones that have been scientifically studied, time-tested, and accredited as being genuine. Some say the recordings sound like a primitive language, while others claim they sound more like profanities. Other similar recordings have also been made in states such as Ohio, Florida, and Mississippi, as well.

Because these particular recordings DO NOT MATCH any other known species or animals on record, I give these sounds an absolute "10" on my Sasquatch Credibility scale record. In other words, this is THE REAL DEAL, folks!

So, there, we have just covered the main body of evidence to date suggesting there's something more to this Bigfoot phenomenon than meets the eye. But is it concrete, irrefutable evidence of the creature's existence? I'm going to leave that one up to you to decide. Let it be known, however, that in a court of Law, CIRCUMSTANTIAL EVIDENCE, if it is strong enough, meaning if it's "beyond reasonable doubt," may be used to get a conviction of sorts. And most of these points, in my opinion, seem to swing the pendulum in favor of the creature, Sasquatch/Bigfoot, living among us.

JUST SO THE RECORD IS STRAIGHT, the following comments are based strictly upon THE AUTHOR'S OPINION and OBSERVATIONS, not necessarily anyone else's.

SLAM...down goes the gavel in favor of the cryptid, Bigfoot, being out there... SOMEWHERE in the lonely darkness of night or hiding in the remote recesses of a backwoods swamp. Behold, THE SWAMP THING **REALLY DOES EXIST**, folks! He's NOT A MYTHICAL BEING! Another pet name I have for Bigfoot is "THE NIGHT CRAWLER," because the creature is mostly seen at night, rather than during the day. This almost led to me calling the book, *"The Newcomerstown Night Crawler: Evidence of Bigfoot?"*

THE CONCLUSION

Although you have the right to your own opinion, my experiences and encounters with the cryptid called Bigfoot leads me to believe that the being IS ACTUALLY **REAL!** The odds of the creature in my encounters being a mere man dressed up in a monkey suit are so incredibly STAGGERING it defies logic. Men simply CANNOT disappear from off a mountain top without first leaving some sort of sign in the process, nor can they sprint 40 yards in 4 SECONDS FLAT while wearing a huge, bulky bigfoot suit. Then throw into the mix overcoming physical size, an estimated 600 lb. being, plus the ability to see through things and you have the makings of *A Supposed, "PHYSICAL BEING"* that sounds more **SUPERNATURAL** than anything else. Let's face it, over a thousand eyewitnesses over the last 50 years simply **CANNOT** BE ALL WRONG!

Something is out there lurking in the remote shadows of our forests and or hiding in the recesses of a secluded swamp, creek or body of water somewhere that is downright unworldly. Everything in these areas appears normal, that is, until the sun goes down; then it's every man for himself! Why? ***BECAUSE THAT'S WHEN THE CREATURE GOES ON THE PROWL!***

People have literally been 'scared out of their wits' by a large hairy monster tip-toeing around their campfires at night or perhaps peeking around a tree or looking inside a window of their house or trailer. For whatever reason, it seems the cryptid called Bigfoot favors mobile homes or house trailers to hang around. Perhaps it likes these dwellings because they're not as structurally sound as regular houses are and therefore, easier to make loud wrapping noises on. Nevertheless, multiple reports have been made around trailer and mobile home parks; too many to deny the possible connection.

To many, the question IS NOT…"Is Bigfoot or Sasquatch real," but rather "What is this bizarre entity called Bigfoot?" Could he really be a by-product of human evolution? Is he, as some claim, part of a race of Extraterrestrial beings left behind by Aliens at the dawn of civilization? Or perhaps they are demons, ghosts or some type of woodland spirits? Some biblical theorists even believe they could be the holdovers of a forgotten race of Pre-Adamite beings who once lived on the earth before Adam. Other biblical teachers believe they could be supernaturally connected to the race of giants whom the Bible says lived both BEFORE and AFTER the Flood of Noah, as found in Genesis 6:4. And last but not least, certain scientists believe that, if true, the hairy monster could be the *"Missing Link"* referred to in the theory of Evolution.

It seems there are more questions than answers and with little to no actual proof to back any of these theories up with, Bigfoot's existence will continue to remain a mystery. For the record there is evidence (some real, some fake) of the creature's existence. Multiple big footprints have been found in remote sections of the forests, woodlands and fields all over this planet, not just in one isolated area. So if this B.F. phenomenon is fake, then the hoax is worldwide and I think that that, in itself, is unbelievable. Wouldn't you agree?

Along with the famous Bigfoot prints there are also blood, hair and tissue samples, as well, plus a few rare photographs and video clips of the creature. Also, there are some alleged "Yeti" whelps, hollers and screams which have been recorded that don't seem to be indigenous with natural animal calls of the surrounding area. However, as noted, the field of Bigfoot research is so ripe with "fake" evidence that not too many scientist take the phenomenon very seriously. So far to date, those scientists who do, out of curiosity, have yet to find any concrete evidence supporting the creature's existence.

Sightings of this so-called "Mythical Beast" go all the way back to the flood of Noah, as purported in the flood story of Gilgamesh (one of the earliest manuscripts on record). In it, Gilgamesh, the King of

Urak, eventually becomes friends with Enkiduh, a large hairy man first discovered to be living in the forest. Now whether you believe in the Epics of Gilgamesh or not, it's uncanny how the ancient tablets reveal a story about a being resembling Bigfoot.

The actual proof, however, of this creature's existence has been shrouded in mystery down through the ages. For the record, there has never, ever been a body or bones found of a being resembling Sasquatch or Bigfoot. Its existence seems to be more widely supported by eyewitness accounts rather than by hardcore, solid evidence; making any genuine sign questionable, at best. This is why I don't support the theory of an actual, flesh & blood primate, because if this were the case, then we should have already discovered physical evidence of it by now. That's why I lean more towards *the Supernatural aspect* of the elusive being. In my upcoming book entitled, *"BIGFOOT: THE SUPERNATURAL PORTAL & The Biblical Connection"* I will elaborate more upon the evidence supporting my thesis. To say the information I've uncovered in this second book is undeniably interesting, would be an understatement of the highest degree.

We happen to be living in a day and age where the paranormal or supernatural is actually becoming commonplace. With that being said, the entity called Bigfoot/Sasquatch and his other namesakes is only one type of being reported that DOES NOT fit the "quote" normal mindset. There are also other cryptids (so-called "Mythical Beings") out there which have been seen today that defy "normal rationalized thinking" simply because they ARE NOT supposed to exist. In fact, without going into a lot of detail, there is a ranch in the state of Utah that has been dubbed (by its owners) as one of the "scariest" places on earth. This property has been a virtual hotbed of paranormal activity, producing numerous sightings of different cryptids, including Bigfoot.

Plus, UFO activity has also been sighted in the area, as well, perhaps linking the two mysterious phenomenons together. I will touch more upon these things in my upcoming book.

Some people simply don't believe in Sasquatch/Bigfoot because they haven't seen the elusive being for themselves. However, if seeing is your only criteria for believing that something exists, then I'm afraid you're living in a proverbial "little black box." It's HIGH TIME you pull your head out of the sand and start believing in the unseen. Here are some things that are quote "INVISIBLE" to the naked eye that scientists have confirmed as being true and factual:

Atoms, Oxygen, molecules, RNA-DNA, chromosomes, chemicals, etc. and etc. Simply put, without these things life as we know it WOULD NOT EXIST and you and I wouldn't be having this conversation. And last, but certainly, not least, some scientists have come forward and proclaimed that now there is even PROOF and EVIDENCE that GOD HIMSELF IS REAL because of the delicate balance in which our earth exists in our universe.

The bottom line is, just because you can't see something DOES NOT mean that it isn't real. In other words, as I've said multiple times throughout this book, OVER A THOUSAND plus people all over this world *simply* **CANNOT BE ALL WRONG**, period! **SOMETHING IS OUT THERE...SOMEWHERE!** And it's HIGH TIME that B.F. skeptics open up their mind and eyes to that particular possibility!!!

I personally want to THANK YOU for purchasing this book and I pray that it has been a help and a blessing to those of you who, like me, have been searching so desperately for the truth surrounding the Bigfoot mystery. LIKE BIGFOOT, THE TRUTH IS OUT THERE... SOMEWHERE... just waiting to be discovered... PERHAPS BY SOMEONE LIKE YOU............

STAY TUNED... If you think this book has been a bit bizarre, you haven't seen anything, yet! In *"Bigfoot: The Supernatural Portal & The Biblical Connection,"* you will uncover "pertinent" information that will help you unravel the Bigfoot Mystery! But my question to you is, *"Will you be able to handle it?"* As I said, before, STAY TUNED!!!

CHAPTER 10 Footnotes

Ft. 1 *"Finding Big*foot: Everything You Need To Know," By Animal Planet; Back Cover

Ft. 2 www.joshuastevens.net Squatch Watch: 92 Years of Bigfoot Sightings in the US and Canada. Sept. 17, 2013

Ft. 3 www.bfro.net Idaho State University Researcher Coordinates Analysis of Body Imprint That May Belong to a Sasquatch (Last paragraph)

Ft. 4 *"Finding Bigfoot: Everything You Need To Know,"* By *Animal Planet*; pg. 24.

Ft. 5 The Skookum Cast; https://skeptoid.com

Ft. 6 www.animalplanet.com The Evidence For Bigfoot l Finding Bigfoot l Animal Planet

Ft. 7 Ibid; Part 3, paragraph 4

Ft. 8 howstuffworks.com Bigfoot or Monkey Suits and Fake Feet 4th paragraph

Ft. 9 Ibid; Farther down the page from ft. 8.

Ft. 10 http://www.bfro.net/legends/ Pre-Columbian and Early American Legends of Bigfoot-like Beings 1st paragraph

Ft.   11   http://www.ya-native.com/nativeamerica/Bigfoot-SasquatchLegends.html pg. 2 of 3

Ft. 12 http://www.bfro.net/legends/ Pre-Columbian and Early American Legends of Bigfoot-like Beings pg. 3 of 3

Ft. 13 http://www.unexplainedmonsters.com/bigfoot/bigfoot-legend.html The Legend of Bigfoot-Native American Legend Sasquatch pg. 4 of 4 90.

"Feeling brave, I set out following the humongous looking footprints in the snow. Here I was, a mere 12 year old boy ON THE TRAIL of "THE ABOMINABLE SNOWMAN!""

The Author

I'm still ON THE TRAIL of Bigfoot today through the eyes of my readers. This is your chance to "FEEL BRAVE" and act upon it by telling me your story! I have a website going up in a couple of weeks... just GOOGLE "The Ohio Monster" by David Walker and it should take you right to it. And BE BRAVE, I will believe you!!!

About the Author

David Walker grew up in the small town of Newcomerstown, Ohio, a State with a well-known reputation for producing monster whitetails. David's father taught him the basics of hunting & fishing, but it was his uncle Homer who taught him the skills necessary to effectively hunt big mature bucks. Because of this relationship with his uncle, David ended up spending lots of time in the outdoors which led to some of his encounters with the large hairy monster known as Bigfoot.

It was also around this same time period that David had gotten saved during a revival at his church. This ultimately developed into a lifelong pursuit of studying the Holy Bible, which (among other things) eventually led to some invaluable research on the cryptid called Bigfoot/Sasquatch. This culminated into some fascinating material about the subject which will soon be showcased in his next book entitled, *"Bigfoot: The Supernatural Portal & The Biblical Connection."*

Today, the author lives in Atlanta, Ga, with his beautiful wife, Barb McCarter Walker (Author of *"Panther and Me,"* Book Art Press) and their three Service dogs Nala, Oreo and Sasha. Sasha, the smallest is also called "The Little Big Boss," because she is the oldest and (according to her) the wisest one, as well...lol! Currently, David is a full-time Security Officer, by profession. However, with only 4 more years left to retirement, he's looking forward to spending more time with his wife and also being able to enjoy the great outdoors again like he did as a child. And who knows, perhaps he'll even have another encounter or two with... *The Thing,* again...you never know!!!

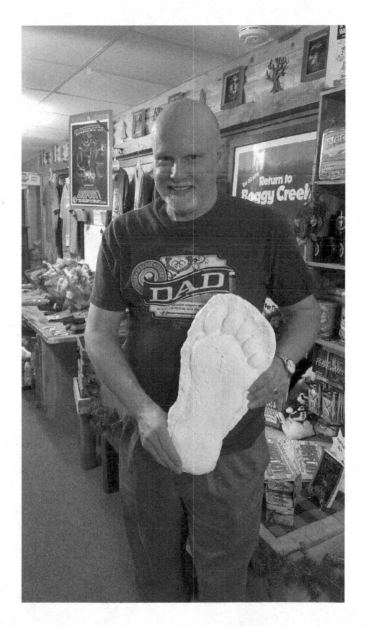

David Walker standing in "Expedition Bigfoot, The Sasquatch Museum" located in Cherry Log, Ga. The author is holding a replica of a Bigfoot print taken by Sheriff deputy Dennis Heryford (found in chp. 10 of this book). The immense track measured 15 inches long & 6 inches wide. Plus, several strands of hair were also found with these tracks, as well.